SELF MADE

NELY GALÁN

with GUY GARCIA

SPIEGEL & GRAU · NEW YORK

SELF MADE

.

Becoming Empowered, Self-Reliant, and Rich in Every Way

Published in the United States by Spiegel & Grau, an imprint of Random House, a division of Penguin Random House LLC, New York.

Spiegel & Grau and Design is a registered trademark of Penguin Random House LLC.

LIBRARY OF CONGRESS CATALOGING-IN-PUBLICATION DATA
Names: Galan, Nely.
Title: Self made : becoming empowered, self-reliant, and rich in every way / Nely Galan.
Description: New York : Spiegel & Grau, [2016]
Identifiers: LCCN 2016007226| ISBN 9780812989755 (hardback) | ISBN 9780812989762 (ebook)
Subjects: LCSH: Self-realization in women. | Success in business. | Success. | Wealth. | Entrepreneurship. | BISAC: SELF-HELP / Personal Growth / Success. | BUSINESS & ECONOMICS / Motivational.
Classification: LCC HQ1206 .G347 2016 | DDC 650.1—dc23
LC record available at http://lccn.loc.gov/2016007226

Printed in the United States of America on acid-free paper

randomhousebooks.com
spiegelandgrau.com

2 4 6 8 9 7 5 3 1

First Edition

Book design by Barbara M. Bachman

To my parents, Arsenio and Nelida,

who sacrificed everything to bring me to this country

and to whom I owe my self-made journey.

Los quiero mucho. I love you both very much.

■

To Brian, who entered my life while we were both working

on becoming self-made inside and who has brought only

light, love, and generosity into my life. You are the most

considerate and loving person I know. I love and

appreciate you. Thank you for loving my son and being the

best dad in the world, which has allowed me to soar.

■

To my son, Lukas. You are my love.

You have made my life rich in every way.

I pass the self-made torch to you.

I know you have it in you!

You will recognize her on sight,

for She is a woman

who looks just like you

and all that you love.

Remember?

—FROM *UNTIE THE STRONG WOMAN*
BY CLARISSA PINKOLA ESTÉS

Traveler, there is no trail.

You blaze the trail as you go.

—ANTONIO MACHADO

foreword

■

SUZE ORMAN

WHEN NELY ASKED ME IF I'D BE WILLING TO WRITE a foreword for her book, the only question I asked was "What's it called?" "*Self Made*," she said. And that was enough for me to say yes.

I've known Nely for a long time. We have some very good mutual friends, including the amazing Nell Merlino, the woman who started Take Our Daughters to Work Day and is the founder and president of Count Me In for Women's Economic Independence, a national organization dedicated to helping women entrepreneurs. I've always liked Nely—she's spirited and energetic and authentic—and admired her journey from Cuban Jersey girl to woman of power in the entertainment business. She never forgot her roots, she served her community, and, it seemed to me, she achieved success on her own terms, without compromise. We both share an unlikely road to success from humble origins—I grew up on the South Side of Chicago and worked as a waitress until I was thirty. But it wasn't until I learned exactly how Nely became self-made, which she reveals in this book, that my admiration for her soared. Who knew she was a real estate tycoon? Who knew she had been so smart and strategic with her money and that was what gave her the power to control her destiny?

Nely embodies so many of the truths I've been teaching women over the past twenty-five years. We share a philosophy about money. She understands that only you can save yourself. She understands that it's up to you to value yourself—I say, "Don't put yourself on sale!" She says, "Choose yourself!" I ask you to live below your means; she urges you to think like an immigrant. We both love the word "sacrifice." To own your power, I say, "Say your name!" Nely says, "Declare yourself!" We share a belief in what it truly means to be rich in every way.

In my book *Women & Money* I have a chapter called "The 8 Qualities of a Wealthy Woman." I'd like to offer a passage from that book as a wish for you, the reader of Nely's book, who is on her way toward becoming self-made.

Remember to muster up your courage and silence your
   fear.

Remember to keep your eye on the goal, on what you
   really want to accomplish, no matter what anyone
   says or does to deter you. Just keep moving ahead.

Remember to stay involved with your money, to nurture a healthy relationship with it, for what happens to your money affects the quality of your life
   and the lives of all those you love.

Remember always to do what is right rather than what
   is easy, and never put yourself on sale, because you
   deserve better than that.

Last but not least, I ask you to look everyone you meet
   straight in the eye and with the force and power of
   all the women in the world behind you, within you,
   and in front of you, SAY YOUR NAME.

Self-Made is a movement whose time has come. I am
proud to be on the front lines alongside my friend Nely and
in solidarity with all of you.

—Suze

contents

3.

HOW TO BECOME
SELF-MADE   137

introduction

■

I **AM SELF-MADE. WHAT A POWERFUL THING TO BE ABLE**
to say. Especially as a woman and as one who was not born in
this country, who was not (until recently) a college graduate,
who did not have an obvious skill or talent, and who did not
invent a multibillion-dollar product. I am an ordinary woman
who has had an extraordinary life, not because I went to the
right schools or had connections, but because I took success
and happiness into my own hands and became financially
self-reliant by thinking like an entrepreneur.

To be able to say "I am self-made" is an honor. To be self-
made is a new way of defining success for women. A self-

made woman is free because she is financially independent and on her way. A self-made woman acts as if she has an owner's stake in every aspect of her life—because she does. A self-made woman is empowered, self-reliant, and rich in every way.

Becoming self-made does not have to be a grandiose feat. You don't have to look up to find a self-made woman. Just look around you. She's the stay-at-home mom with a baby who runs an online boutique out of her apartment; the cleaning lady who books through her website and charges through PayPal; the freelance nurse who processes payments through Square; the franchise owner who employs her whole family; the corporate employee who sells her jewelry designs on Etsy; the empty nester who rents out rooms in her house through Airbnb; the baker who promotes her one-of-a-kind cakes on Instagram; the woman who makes Vine videos for corporations with her teenage child; the millennial who is paying off college by driving for Uber. These are all some of the women I have met on the road over the past four years, they are the embodiment of becoming self-made, and they are the inspiration for this book. These women are changing the economic future for themselves, for their families, and for generations to come. Self-made is a call to action, and it is a leap forward in the economic evolution of women. This is our moment to choose empowerment.

Never before in history has living an entrepreneurial life been more attainable for all of us. The digital age has revolutionized our ability to get started; you don't need much more than a smart phone or a computer. You can start a business from your home, in your pajamas. You don't have to quit your job. And you don't have to do it alone! You can get your kids to help because they're already good at social media (and as a fringe benefit, they're less likely to grow up entitled). You can enlist your husband or a friend and pool your resources and talents.

Here is my wish for you: I want you to live a rich life in every way. Rich in money, rich in family, rich in love, rich in time—abundant! It's not just about having money, but financial empowerment is where it begins. It means getting out of survival mode. It means getting out of that state where you are just one problem away from financial catastrophe. It means changing your mindset from instant gratification to goal orientation. In time, it means being able to work because you want to and not because you have to. It means being able to reward yourself and your children with things like an education, trips, and owning a home. It means being able to sleep at night without worry.

We are told that money doesn't buy happiness. Don't get me wrong: I absolutely believe that's true! Money should never be an end in itself. But until you are financially self-reliant, you are not truly free. There is no true empowerment until you have your own money. I am not telling you to quit your job and start the next Zappos—at least not right away. But I am going to show you how to think like an entrepreneur and an owner in the job you have now, no matter what you do.

Self-made is about having a dream, and the desire and discipline to work toward that dream. I have to tell you: One of

SELF
MADE

THERE IS NO TRUE
EMPOWERMENT
UNTIL YOU HAVE
YOUR OWN
MONEY.

.

my favorite words is "sacrifice." I know I can convince you that buying things to make yourself happy doesn't even work in the short term. You have to put your money where it can grow so that you can make your dreams come true. Once you do this, you will be able to move on to bigger ideas and even bigger dreams.

Self-made is a state of mind, and it's about thinking even bigger than getting a good job, or a promotion, or the corner office, because you can have these things and still not be self-made, or feel self-made inside. When you embrace the self-made mindset, you will not feel victimized or disappointed, because you're taking power into your own hands, and you understand that no one else can do it for you. You are the captain of your ship. You make your own success. *You* determine your own value, not a man, or a boss, or a corporation.

I've learned in my life that the only person you can change is yourself. And when you change yourself and are fully in your power, people around you change because a grounded and secure aura emanates from you, without the need to say anything, without having to be aggressive or off-putting. You send a message that says, *I am complete. I am not going to allow you to treat me in a way that I don't deserve.*

In this book, I want to teach you everything I wish I had known when I was younger. I'll share some advice and guidance—with a few secrets and tricks thrown in. With the help of some amazing women (and a few men), I've also created a website—becomingSELFMADE.com—that houses an incredible amount of information and resources to anticipate and answer your questions, give you the tools you need to crunch the numbers, and put you in touch with organizations that can help in a wide variety of ways. And if I've done my job right, you will be inspired to start an entrepreneurial business or project that you own—right now!

My personal goal for every one of you is to make it to the finish line—to create a life that is rich in every way, to build a secure future for you and your family, to sleep peacefully at night.

The scholar Joseph Campbell wrote about "the hero's journey"—a classic storyline in which the hero embarks on an adventure, faces trials and adversity, triumphs over them, and returns home transformed. I want you to recognize that right here, right now, as you read this book, you are at the start of this process. You are embarking on a heroine's journey, a quest that is about choosing yourself, putting yourself to the test, reaping the rewards of your new way of life, changing your view of what's possible, achieving your dreams, and then passing the torch to your children and your community. Because one of the greatest rewards of a self-made life is seeing how the sparks from your personal revolution can light a fire in others. When you become self-made, you become an evangelist for the cause; you want to spread the gospel of self-reliance and help others get there too. So come—let's begin. The revolution starts inside of you.

—Nely

I.

:

MY STORY.
YOUR STORY.
OUR STORY.

WHEN I ARRIVED IN THIS COUNTRY FROM CUBA as a little girl, the United States had just come through the women's movement of the 1960s. Gloria Steinem, the inspirational activist and founder of *Ms.* magazine, was its iconic leader. Of course, as a child learning how to navigate a new culture, I wasn't aware of the dramatic societal changes taking place. All I knew was that this country offered my family a safe place to begin our lives again—a land of opportunity and political freedom. We had control over our destiny, the power of self-determination. With hard work and sacrifice, we could build a better life, as generations of immigrants did before us. We could vote and have a voice and be heard. No one was going to come and take our homes and everything we'd worked for away from us. I learned from an early age the importance of self-sufficiency.

As I grew up and got an education, I learned more about the advances and opportunities forged by feminist pioneers like Steinem—politicians and writers and journalists who inspired so many courageous women to break through boundaries and fight for equal rights at home and in the workplace. Despite the strong, traditional values I was raised with as a Latina—and the sometimes old-fashioned ideas of what a young woman should and should not do—the women's movement resonated with me on an emotional and intellectual level. As an immigrant, I understood that this was the greatest country in the world for women, and I deeply appreciated it and wanted to take full advantage of the opportunities I had.

From a young age, out of necessity, I took on adult responsibilities in the household. My parents arrived in the United States with nothing—we'd left behind our home and all of our possessions—and we started over. As kids do, I adapted much more quickly than the adults, and I understood that it was my duty to help my parents in ways that are familiar to many children of immigrants.

I started working when I was thirteen years old—you'll hear about my first experience with entrepreneurship in a little while—and learned some tough lessons along the way. Luckily, I had some excellent mentors; some of them may not even realize to this day that I consider them mentors! I studied them closely and emulated the traits and techniques that I saw as instrumental to their success. I learned from my failures too—and trust me, there were plenty of them—and took away many valuable lessons in the process.

I went from unpaid intern to TV news producer to television station management. I started a TV production business that failed for four years before I remade it (with a good hard shove from a mentor) and it took off. I became the first Latina president of a TV network, produced over seven hundred shows in English and Spanish, and appeared on *The Celebrity Apprentice*. I worked hard every step of the way and made money. The key to my story is that even when I was making money, I sacrificed, I did not live large, and I invested my money in real estate. In time, the income from my real estate business meant that I didn't have to work anymore; I could live very comfortably off the income from my investments. And that gave me freedom—the freedom to do the work I *wanted* to do, not work I *had* to do—and what I wanted was work that would nourish me creatively and intellectually and spiritually.

When I realized I was financially free to pursue whatever I wanted, first I screamed and cried! I couldn't believe it! And then I realized I had some unfinished business to attend to. So I went back to school, finished my BA, and then spent four years getting a graduate degree in psychology. I worked on my emotional baggage. I cleaned house in my mind. I came to terms with a lot of stuff about my heritage, my culture, my feminine side, everything. These were essential steps in my self-made journey, and they allowed me to become the kind of role model I wanted to be for my son. (Now he can't complain about school and homework, because he's seen me powering through it at age forty-five!)

Once I had my degree, I realized that my most meaningful success had come from financial self-reliance, and I wanted to teach that to other women. So in 2012, I started a nonprofit, the Adelante Movement (theadelantemovement.com), a live event and digital learning platform that would empower women and train them in entrepreneurship. In Spanish, *adelante* is a great word; it means "move it! now! let's go!" I crossed the country, speaking initially to my community of Latinas, a group I knew well, but in time others started showing up, first women of color and then all women. It became clear to me that women were looking to connect with each other. They were hungry for information and hungry to build bridges to other women in their communities. That's when I knew that women needed to know that the self-made revolution was well under way and it is only getting stronger.

SELF-MADE IS
A REVOLUTION

. . . .

GLORIA STEINEM RECENTLY TOLD AN INTERVIEWER, "I WISH I had known then what I know now, which is that the women's movement was really an entrepreneurial movement." I think what Steinem means is that without the ability to be whole and financially secure on your own terms, there can be no freedom and no liberation.

I have spent four years crossing the country, and I've met over 100,000 women. What I see happening out there is the beginning of a genuine revolutionary shift: We are in the era of fully empowered women in the do-it-yourself economy.

There are no barriers to entry. The tools of instant entrepreneurship and self-reliance are all around us, and most of them are simple to use and easy to afford. Technology, social media, and the non-centralized shared economy have made it easier than ever to start a business. A new women's movement is rising around financial self-reliance and ownership, because there is no true empowerment as a woman until you have your own money.

Four decades after the original women's movement rocked the culture, the economic crash of 2008 would create a new reality for millions of women who were pushed into becoming the heads of households after their husbands and fathers lost their jobs. These women had to step it up! Out of necessity, Latinas, African Americans, Asians, and Middle Eastern women led the charge as the fastest-growing segment of entrepreneurs and a tremendous economic force in this country. Among women, Latinas are the number one emerging market in the United States, and along with other multiculturals (African Americans, Asian Americans, Native Americans, and women of Middle Eastern descent) they represent the largest growth engine in the U.S. economy. Similarly, around the world, in the BRIC nations (Brazil, Russia, India, and China) and in countries with emerging economies in Africa and the Middle East, in spite of the challenges posed by religious and political obstacles, population sizes, and daunting competition, women are rising up and becoming entrepreneurs for the sake of their children and families. Because of these economic shifts, women today, from many different cultures and backgrounds, are united in a quest for a new financial future, one they can control.

Look around; we have so many role models in public life to inspire us, women who have continued the empowerment conversation started by Steinem and linked it to our financial lives. Sheryl Sandberg, the COO of Facebook, has ignited the idea of "leaning in," coaching women to push aside barriers that keep them out of leadership roles—or as I put it, acting as an owner in your career. Arianna Huffington, who, after a very public divorce and a failed political campaign—two things that might have sidelined a lesser woman—had the idea to create a collective news blog, raised the money, and launched *The Huffington Post,* which is now, just a little over a decade later, a major, influential media company. Then there is the extraordinary Suze Orman, who woke us up to the fact that our emotional lives and our financial lives are inextricably linked and that only by controlling our money do we have the power to control our destiny.

Forbes magazine recently published a cover story about America's richest self-made women that features a range of fascinating, accomplished women, including Jin Sook Chang, who immigrated to the United States from South Korea and worked odd jobs before founding, with her husband, the now multibillion-dollar clothing chain Forever 21.

In pop culture too, some of the most successful actors, musicians, and performers are thinking like entrepreneurs. Oprah crushed the glass ceiling for multicultural women first with *The Oprah Winfrey Show,* a twenty-five-year juggernaut that remade daytime television, and then with her production studio, Harpo, and then with OWN, her network. Taylor Swift took on Apple and the music industry to protect the value of her work. Bethenny Frankel leveraged her reality TV platform to create the Skinnygirl brand. Jessica Alba turned her concerns about the safety of products for her baby into the multimillion-dollar Honest brand of natural products. And the Kardashian matriarch, Kris Jenner, built an empire around her family by monetizing their celebrity via reality TV, social media, and endorsements. Andy Cohen, talk show host and executive producer of the *Real Housewives* franchise, says, "Nobody just wants to be an actress anymore. Today, every woman I meet wants to be identified as a businesswoman, a mogul." It's a sign of the times.

For most women, though, a rich life is not about being famous and wealthy and powerful for its own sake. The higher reward of success for women is being able to bring abundance back to the people they love—their families and their communities. Our mission is about creating a better life for our kids, getting them better schooling, having a house that is paid off, even going back to school ourselves.

Self-Made is a movement that is about being *for* something, not against it. It is a defining moment for women based on economic empowerment. It is a movement that hits on every level: personal, communal, cultural, political. It is inclusive, supportive, collaborative. It is entrepreneurship for the rest of us.

SELF-MADE IS THE
NEW TICKING CLOCK

. . . .

THE SELF-MADE MOVEMENT SPEAKS TO EVERY WOMAN WHO wants to control her destiny and get out of survival mode. It's for women who want a backup plan because they know that they could be laid off from their corporate job tomorrow. It's for women who have devoted their careers to service or to running nonprofits, without a thought for their financial futures. It's for women who have served their country in government jobs or the military and are looking ahead, uncertain about the next chapter in their lives. It's for those of us who feel that there is creativity and greatness in us, but we just need a little help getting started. It's for recent college graduates who are saddled with debt and who can't believe that their high-cost education barely got them an entry-level job. And it's for all of us who haven't been able to follow that traditional, linear career path for one reason or another—maybe because we are immigrants who have had to support our families, or maybe we've had to juggle money and career with raising children or taking care of aging parents. Self-made is for women who may not relate to the obstacles and demands of climbing the corporate ladder, because they are too busy trying to make ends meet. And for the women who are climbing that ladder, it is a call to arms for cultivating an entrepreneurial attitude that will help you advance in your career and will also serve you well on the day that your industry is disrupted and you wake up without a job.

I like to tell the women I speak to that "self-made is the new ticking clock." It's not about *whether* you're going to become self-made; it's about *when* you're going to become self-made. The road to becoming self-made isn't linear or one-size-fits-all. It will be different for each one of you. Some of you will sprint ahead, and some will take your time. Some of the work will come easily, and some of it will require extra focus and effort. Some changes will happen immediately, and others will take patience to realize. You can't do everything at once. But you can start right now.

This book is an invitation. Join us—join this movement. If you're afraid, do it anyway. We were all afraid to take that first step. I'll do my best to inspire you to embrace the fear, because there is no growth without courage. I'll tell you stories of women just like you who took the reins in their lives and never looked back, women who ignited their entrepreneurial spirit with life-changing results. Women are banding together to share resources and collaborate in countless brilliant ways, partnering to start businesses together, and lending a hand to the next generation of self-made women who will follow in their footsteps. This is a chance for you to add your story to theirs.

BEFORE YOU BEGIN, here are a few important questions for you to consider:

- What do you really want out of life?
- What are your goals?

- Who or what in your life has disappointed you?
- Where are you stuck?
- What is your biggest fear about the future?
- What are your greatest dreams? (Dream big!)
- What are you waiting for?

A life-changing journey awaits you. Take my hand. Now. Here. Let's go! *¡Adelante!*

2.

—

IF I KNEW THEN
WHAT I KNOW
NOW . . . WAIT!
I DO KNOW
NOW!

.

LESSONS I'VE LEARNED
ON THE WAY
TO BECOMING
SELF-MADE

there is no prince charming.

ONE OF MY FAVORITE WAYS TO GIVE MYSELF A treat is to spend an hour at Drybar, a franchise founded by the savvy entrepreneur Alli Webb. Drybars are to women what sports bars are to men—a place to unwind, except at Drybar you get your hair blow-dried and you come out looking gorgeous. But like a sports bar, it's a communal experience; some women even make a party of it and book appointments together. Romantic comedies play silently on a loop on big flat-screen TVs (there are subtitles, but, honestly, the words are hardly necessary), and all the women are getting their hair done and chatting/yelling over the din of the hair dryers. What could be better? So picture me, sitting in the lemon-yellow salon chairs as a stylist works on my hair, with tears streaming down my face, and it's a good cry. Without fail, as soon as they get to the part in the movie where the guy is running through the airport to catch the girl and declare his undying love for her, I break down. It gets me every time, even without sound. I can't help it.

I have a screenwriter friend who actually writes these romantic comedies for a living. He told me, "You know those endings where the guy is racing through the airport and he finds the girl seconds before she boards the plane, and then they live happily ever after? Guess what? No real guy would ever do that. I write those scenes because I know they're what women want to see. It's every woman's fantasy."

But even knowing that, I still cry. It's as if there is something encoded in me as a woman that makes me want to believe in the fantasy—that Prince Charming (or Matthew McConaughey) is willing to go to the ends of the earth (or the airport) to swoop in and rescue me. No matter that I am a successful, independent woman; I fully admit there is a part of me that responds to that Prince Charming fantasy. I know it's a cliché, but it's real. I just can't help it.

Why are we talking about Prince Charming in a book about entrepreneurship and financial empowerment? Because what I've confessed above is not unique to me. As I've traveled the country meeting women of all ages and backgrounds, they tell me some version of this fantasy. It sounds corny and old-fashioned, but Prince Charming comes in many modern guises. Maybe Prince Charming is a man who solves all your problems. But maybe Prince Charming is a dream job or a great boss who—*finally!*—recognizes your star potential. Whatever form the rescue fantasy takes, it plays off a lesson we've been taught since childhood—namely, if we play the good girl and work hard, someone is going to recognize how amazing we are and make everything okay. That man or woman or situation will come along and deliver us to the life we've always wanted.

I will tell you, as someone who is still susceptible emotionally to the lure of this fantasy, that it is in fact dangerous. When we rely on someone else to make our dreams come true, we actually give up our dreams. By holding out for some other person, or some situation, or some external thing to make you happy and deliver you to the life you want, you give up your personal power. You will be waiting and waiting, living out this pattern again and again in all its various forms.

The Prince Charming fantasy doesn't just occur in romantic or professional relationships. It can come into play with our parents and even our kids. The women who buy into this fantasy carry around unmet expectations of their mates, their parents, and their children. They end up resentful and disappointed and paralyzed, unable to move forward. When we're trapped in this pattern, we consciously or unconsciously blame others for our inability to take action. We blame the man who hurt us, or the boss who doesn't appreciate us or who won't give us that raise we deserve, or our kid who left home and hardly calls anymore, or our parents who didn't give us what we needed growing up. Someone is always standing in the way of our best future, someone we expected something from who didn't come through.

SELF
MADE

WHEN WE RELY ON SOMEONE ELSE TO MAKE OUR DREAMS COME TRUE, WE ACTUALLY GIVE UP OUR DREAMS.

Our resentments make us behave like victims. But in order to empower ourselves, we have to stop making excuses. We have to stop blaming those around us. We have to take action instead of waiting for someone to bail us out. Have you ever met a person who is waiting for a big inheritance? Or someone who is convinced she'll get rich by playing the lottery every week? Are these people happy? Are they accomplishing great things? It's very unlikely. Because when you live this way, you are living day by day in a holding pattern, waiting for someone else to hand you your life's work on a platter instead of doing it yourself. And you end up stuck and depressed, wondering how much you might have achieved if only you'd been able to take action.

WE HAVE TO KILL PRINCE CHARMING. WE HAVE TO KILL THE FANTASY BECAUSE IT KEEPS US SMALL.

. . . .

IT MIGHT SURPRISE YOU TO HEAR THAT FOR MANY YEARS I WAS waiting for Prince Charming. I was working my way up as a TV producer, I had all the hallmarks of a young professional on the rise. Magazines profiled me as "one to watch," a powerful young Latina who looked as if she had it all—her own company, influential mentors, a voice in the male-dominated entertainment industry. There were splashy photographs of me in cute clothes driving a sports car, posing with confidence. A lot of people would have said that I had it all, but I didn't think so, because I didn't have the perfect man in my life. I grew up watching *telenovelas,* Spanish soap operas that were all about women waiting to be chosen by the perfect man. I'm not making excuses, but these shows are reflective of the culture I was raised in. To my traditional Latino parents, my career success didn't make up for the fact that I didn't have a husband and kids. I felt as if I had failed epically in my personal life, and this feeling began to spread to other parts of my life. Even after all I'd achieved, I was still looking for someone else to confirm my value.

Sometimes you have to hit bottom on a belief to finally bury it and leave it behind. Sometimes an incredibly painful moment becomes the catalyst that blows apart a fantasy in order for a new way of thinking to be born. That's what happened to me. In my twenties and early thirties, I dated a lot of guys who weren't right for me. I also dated a lot of guys who were great, but I always broke up with the great guys before they had a chance to break up with me—an impulse, I see now, that came from my own feelings of inadequacy. A kind of "you can't fire me, I quit" pattern of behavior. None of my romantic relationships lasted very long. Then, one day, I fell madly in love with a Latino guy who was a successful and well-known artist. I had a great career myself, but somehow, throughout our entire relationship, my career came second. I told myself I'd found the perfect guy, and that was more important to me than everything I had accomplished. We were together, more or less, for ten years, and eventually I got pregnant and gave birth to my son. But not long after, I had to confront the fact that we had some deep, irreconcilable differences over fundamental values. Still, the day he left, I was totally devastated. I was thirty-six years old, a grown woman who had run a TV network, and I actually remember thinking, "This guy was supposed to be my dream man! And now I'm a single mom! How did this happen to me?" The fantasy of my perfect Latino family was over. And I blamed myself for letting it happen to me. I couldn't get past the thought that I was doomed to be single forever, because in my culture single mothers don't get the respect they deserve.

I sank into a postpartum depression. I couldn't see the good things in my life, the blessings, only darkness. My *gringa* friend Karen, a filmmaker, came over to visit and found me in a panic.

"What's going to happen to me?" I asked her. "How am I going to raise my son alone? And how am I going to take care of him?"

Karen was baffled. And then she told me to snap out of it! She sat me down and reminded me of all of my accomplishments, my good decisions, and the financial hurdles I'd overcome. She took the time to review my finances, actually showing me in black and white all that I had earned and saved through my own hard work. She smiled and said, "Look at what you've done! You are totally capable. Look at how much money you've made! Look at how you've saved and invested! *You* are effin' Prince Charming!"

And in that moment, I finally saw it for myself. I'd been looking for fulfillment in the wrong place. I didn't need anybody to rescue me. *I was my own Prince Charming.* This realization was a life-changing moment for me. It forced me to look within, to see all that I had created and had yet to create simply by virtue of my strength, my skills, my energy and determination. When I'd been on the hunt for Prince Charming, I was looking for excitement, but I wasn't grounded in the present or planning for the future. I was looking for someone else to take care of me and complete me, rather than looking inside myself and being brave enough to go after my own dreams. It took me a long time to recognize that this is where true happiness lies.

I tell you this story because I want you to know that you can get there too, no matter how tough your current situation seems. You can pull yourself out of this mindset and get un-stuck. You can be your own Prince Charming!

PRINCE CHARMING IS
A RELATIONSHIP KILLER

. . . .

WHEN YOU TURN YOUR LOVE INTEREST INTO THE INSTRUMENT of your personal salvation, you are setting him up to fail, and you are setting yourself up for disappointment. Your partner is human, not a mind-reading alien who is there to make everything better. The truth? Romantic relationships are not unconditional. The closest we come to unconditional love is with our children. But if our mate hurts us, abuses us, cheats on us, or gambles our money away, we need to have options. No one wants to imagine that a relationship will end (let alone end badly), but the fact is that they can and they do.

Therefore, you have to think about cultivating your own money and building your own life and career, even when you are in a relationship that you hope is forever.

We all know that when a relationship ends, it can be incredibly painful. But it is far less painful when you have a career and your own money in the bank. Dealing with the end of a relationship when you have no idea how you are going to support yourself is not a situation you want to be in.

We live in a time of equal partnership, where men and women can share responsibilities at home and at work. There are more and more working moms and stay-at-home dads out there. We have powerful role models like Hillary Clinton and Sonia Sotomayor in politics and public life. The ranks of women who are the breadwinners in their families are growing, and there are countless women blazing trails in their fields. There are more financial and entrepreneurial opportunities for women than ever before, and we live in the country that serves as the model for women's rights around the world. We have no reason to hold on to an outdated fantasy. We can become equal partners to our mates and remain empowered. These are not mutually exclusive concepts.

YOUR BOSS IS NOT YOUR HERO

· · · ·

I HAVE TURNED MANY OF MY BOSSES INTO PRINCE CHARMING BY doting on them, looking up to them, even doing their jobs for them. I did this because I was seeking their recognition and approval. I thought this was the way to get ahead. I was wrong. Sometimes I would get mad enough to say, "You're leaving me with all this work to do over the weekend while you go away on a trip?" But then my boss would cleverly neutralize my anger by saying, "You're so smart. You're so great at your job. What would I do without you?" And for a while, that was enough for me.

I was operating under the tacit and misguided assumption that if I made my boss feel as if he couldn't live without me, I would be rewarded. My thinking went something like this: "If I do this for you, you're going to take care of me." I imagined I wouldn't even need to ask for what I wanted. I would be so very much appreciated I would be rewarded with a big promotion. After all, I'd made myself indispensable. But then, when things didn't happen according to my imagined plan, I would become disappointed and resentful. The power dynamic was actually similar to that of a romantic relationship. When you get into a pattern of seeking approval in a relationship, you relinquish your power and your sense of self. The way to avoid this dynamic is to understand that although you are driven to work hard and do a great job for your boss, you also have to be clear-sighted about your expectations and take responsibility for your success. And at the appropriate moment, you have to tell your boss what you want. If the answer is not what you want to hear, you need to start planning your next move. Even if the answer is encouraging, do not make the mistake of seeing your boss as your savior. It's bad for both of you.

Until I started my own business and became the boss, I

was in a cycle of having high expectations of those around me; then, invariably, I'd be let down and experience abject disappointment. I was blaming others, but then I realized that the common denominator in all of my disappointing relationships was *me*! I realized that the boss is human. Your colleagues have their own issues to deal with, and they have their own boss or an investor or client to answer to. Bosses are not there to save you or to help you work out your issues, your insecurities, or your fears. They need you to do a job and do it well. They will model behavior for you, good or bad, and you've got to learn from that; it's a part of your job. It is also your job to ask for what you want. And it's your responsibility to do what you need to do to grow and prosper and get to the next level. Your boss can't make that happen for you.

DON'T FALL IN LOVE
WITH A COMPANY

· · · ·

I HAVE WORKED FOR SOME SEXY CORPORATIONS—SONY, HBO, Fox. Many people today dream of jobs at cool companies like Apple, Google, and Amazon. But don't make the mistake of becoming enamored of your company and turning it into your Prince Charming, because you can lose sight of your own value and your own needs in the blinding glare of the prestige of Corporation X. Unfortunately, I have many girlfriends who found themselves in this situation, laid off and replaced by a younger, cheaper model after devoting their careers to a single company. The corporation just became another version of the man you have to please every day. Don't let this happen to you!

When you work for a company with a big recognizable name, it's easy to get sucked in. I learned this lesson when I was the president of Telemundo, the Spanish-language TV network then co-owned by Sony. At Telemundo, I was constantly receiving gifts and flowers and invitations, and it was all incredibly seductive; I was seduced by my own job! But as soon as I left that job and went out on my own and was trying to do business without the Sony name, all I had was my own brand; the flowers and the gifts and the invitations stopped overnight. Without the big brand behind me, I was on my own, responsible for my own opportunities and failures. With no big corporation to hide behind, I had to build my own personal brand. It was a painful reality check, but I'm glad I experienced it. Working for a corporation can teach you a lot, but it's like marrying royalty: When things end, you get stripped of your title, and you go home a commoner.

I recently spoke to a group of upper-level executives at a very big corporation. There were three female presidents in the audience, all extremely talented and capable leaders. And I wondered, were these women thinking entrepreneurially about their future? Or were they falling into the trap of thinking that their hot company was Prince Charming? Many corporations do offer attractive stock options, and that stock can end up making you a lot of money. However, if you work in the corporate world, you can't put all your eggs in that basket. The workplace is changing, and it is no longer safe to assume that you will work at the same corporation for twenty or thirty years. If you work in a corporate job, I am going to ask you to engage your entrepreneurial mindset on the side. I am not telling you to cheat on your company. I am just asking you to cultivate owning something for yourself. This doesn't mean that you shouldn't give your all to your job. In fact, learning to think like an owner in your current job is great training for your future business—more on that later.

DON'T MAKE YOUR CHILD
YOUR PRINCE OR PRINCESS

. . . .

THE LOVE BETWEEN A PARENT AND A CHILD IS A BEAUTIFUL thing. I know a lot of parents, especially single moms, who work incredibly hard to give everything to their kids, and then they have a hard time letting them go. I can understand where these parents are coming from. My son is sixteen, and I am already dreading the day he goes off to college. But we have to be careful. Kids from traditional cultures often grow up translating and solving problems for their families. Then parents expect their kids to stick around and take care of them, whether emotionally or physically, instead of living their own lives. When you put this kind of burden on your children, you are not allowing them to fully blossom, and you will eventually create so much guilt that their love turns into duty. This dynamic is not healthy, and it can create a cycle of dysfunction for generations to come. The same dynamic can be true when children become overly dependent on a parent, which doesn't allow them to develop and create their own lives.

HAPPILY EVER AFTER

. . . .

THERE IS A VERY HAPPY ENDING HERE. KILL THE FANTASY, BUT become Prince Charming for yourself. You have everything you need inside you to accomplish this. You can push yourself. You can make yourself proud. You can forgive yourself for past mistakes, and you can have financial independence and your own dreams. This does not mean that you are destined to be alone. It doesn't mean that you have to break up with your boyfriend or leave your husband. As human beings, we exist in relationships. We need other people!

Years after the devastating breakup with my son's father, a friend showed up in my life who was interested in me and in helping me raise my son. At first, I resisted his overtures; he was too nice, too normal, and I was used to drama. But thank God I had killed the Prince Charming fantasy and was ready to be in a grown-up relationship. Brian and I have now been together for eleven years. When they meet Brian and see how kind he is, people say, "You're so lucky that you found him." As if I won the lottery. To which I respond, "Well, he is great, but to tell you the truth, we're both lucky! I was already Princess Charming when we met. I'd gone to therapy. I'd made money and invested it. I was a baked cake." It's easier to find a great mate when you are complete and self-reliant. We were two people coming together who were grown up, had done their own work, and were committed to working on a relationship one day at a time. No Prince Charming fantasy here.

When you lose the fantasy, the expectations you have of your relationships are going to change, because now you know that you can count on yourself 100 percent of the time, so your relationships are the icing on the cake. You are the only one with the ability to make yourself feel complete. When you free yourself from the notion of needing someone else to make everything right, you will become everything that you ever want from someone else.

We all have moments of doubt. It's only human to get scared, no matter who you are or where you are on your path. The rescue fantasy is stubborn and recurring. You go back to your old mindset of victimization and jealousy. You want to quit. But you have to talk yourself down and give yourself credit. *This is not easy. But it's worth it.* Mindfulness will bring you back. This is why I preach that self-made is a daily practice.

This is the beginning of it all. This is the internal shift we need to make in order to get on the road to being self-made. Once you've shifted your thinking and embraced the self-made mindset, the next stop is money. Not because money is the be-all and end-all in life, but because financial empowerment and self-reliance ground you and set the tone for how you will allow yourself to be treated, for how you walk in the world, for how you will find your own power, and for how that power will help you deal with any obstacle that comes your way.

EXERCISE:

Are You Waiting to Be Rescued?

Think about the places in your life where the Prince Charming fantasy may be playing out:

- o   your romantic partner
- o   your boss
- o   your company/institution/school
- o   the government/military
- o   your parent
- o   your child

Ask yourself the following questions:

- o   What are your unmet expectations?
- o   What resentments are you holding?
- o   What traits do certain people or institutions possess that make you feel that they can save you?

exercise

o   Can you cultivate those qualities within
    yourself and make them your own?
o   What do you need to do to take personal
    responsibility for your own happiness?
o   Are you willing to change your relationship
    with your Prince Charming—whoever or
    whatever it may be—in order to become
    self-made?

It may be helpful to write your responses to
these questions and any thoughts that the exer-
cises in this book provoke in a dedicated self-made
notebook or journal. I find it helps me process my
experiences by writing them down and cultivates
self-awareness in general. Don't be self-conscious:
No one is grading you; this is a private act. Don't
worry about making your writing perfect. Just be
honest with yourself, or as honest as you can be at
the time. You might, down the road, look back and
have insights gained from perspective you've acquired.

think like an immigrant.

MMIGRANTS ARE NATURAL-BORN ENTREPRENEURS, AND there is a lot to be learned from them. Did you know that most entrepreneurs in America are immigrants or first generation? In 2010, more than 40 percent of Fortune 500 companies were founded by immigrants or by the children of immigrants. Although they make up 13 percent of the U.S. population, immigrants are responsible for a quarter of all new businesses. Research conducted by EthniFacts shows that immigrants in the United States consistently exceed the rest of the population in optimism and in aspiration to reinvent themselves through hard work and entrepreneurialism.

They understand the self-made mindset out of necessity; it's also a way of coping with the inevitable ups and downs of life.

The truth is that bad stuff is going to happen in your life. We want to deny it. We want to protect our kids from it. We want to believe, *My kid is never going to feel the pain of failure or struggle*. We think that somehow we can prevent it. And that, in fact, is ridiculous. You are inevitably going to experience setbacks and failures, and the more prepared you are for them, the better off you'll be. This is where immigrants have the advantage. Often the very reason they've immigrated is because of a traumatic or devastating experience in their homeland that no one expected. Maybe their country's economy failed, or the banking system was corrupt and they couldn't even claim their savings. In my case, the Communist revolution in Cuba meant that my family left as fast as we could, with only the shirts on our backs. We had to leave everything behind. Can you imagine that kind of pain?

In America, we tend to live with this kind of irrational notion that we will always be taken care of and that everything is going to be okay in the end. But then the unexpected happens. Maybe it's a natural disaster that destroys your home, or a medical issue that drains your resources, or your company downsizes and you lose your job. We can't necessarily prevent such things from happening, but we can lessen the damage by being financially prepared. It doesn't mean these setbacks won't be incredibly tough to deal with. But it is much harder to lose your home with no insurance. It is much harder to lose your job when you don't have money put away somewhere for a rainy day. It is much harder to go through the pain of a divorce when you've never worked a day in your life and were financially dependent on your spouse.

Immigrants don't subscribe to magical thinking. They tend to be more resilient and determined to bounce back from setbacks and to do a lot with a little because they understand that uncertainty is a part of life. That's why I say you have to stop thinking in survival mode. Survival mode means you are living paycheck to paycheck or, even worse, living off someone else's paycheck. Then some catastrophic thing happens in your life, and you find yourself defenseless, hopeless. Maybe even homeless. Don't wait until a catastrophic moment in your life forces you to reality check your magical thinking.

Thomas Friedman is a three-time Pulitzer Prize–winning author and a columnist for *The New York Times*. In his 2011 book, *That Used to Be Us,* he encourages Americans to get back in touch with their immigrant spirit by looking to the values and attitudes of immigrants as a guiding light. When we harness this mentality, we can do great things.

THE WORLD'S YOUNGEST AVON LADY

• • • •

THE PATH TO SELF-RELIANCE IS DIFFERENT FOR EVERY WOMAN. In my case, the journey began at a very young age. My family came to the United States from Cuba when I was five years old and my brother was three. In 1959, Fidel Castro and his rebels overthrew the government and instituted a Communist regime. Private property was seized, those loyal to the previous government were put on trial and imprisoned, and socialist policies were forcibly put in place. Suddenly we were living under a military dictatorship. Hundreds of thousands of Cubans fled for the United States in search of greater political and economic freedom. Among them were my parents, who'd lost everything they had worked to build—their home, their possessions, all of it had to be handed over to the government.

My parents were in their thirties when we arrived in this country. They had to learn a new language and create new identities for themselves. They had to rebuild their lives. It was a complete reboot for them. They worked humbly at anything and everything and struggled to make ends meet. My dad, who had owned supermarkets and car dealerships back in Cuba, painted cars on the assembly line at Ford Motors. My mom had a college degree but took work as a seamstress in a factory. To earn extra money, she would make wedding dresses from home and babysit all the kids in the neighborhood. My parents, by example, imparted a strong work ethic, discipline, humility, and gratitude. They never complained about what had happened to them. They loved their new country, and they taught my brother and me to love it and to be grateful every day for being here.

We settled in Teaneck, New Jersey, a predominantly Jewish and African American community where we were the only Latino family on our block. We struggled to make ends meet. I realized early that my parents needed my help—with the new language they were learning, for one thing—and that I needed to be self-sufficient. It's common for immigrant kids to grow up feeling a sense of responsibility for their parents and wanting to help them. But my freshman year of high school, something began to change in me—a shift to a more courageous and confident version of myself. I was a good student at an all-girls Catholic school that my parents really couldn't afford. One night I overheard them talking when they thought I was asleep.

"*¡Dios!*" my mother said. "How are we going to pay for this school?"

"Don't worry," my father said. "Jesus is going to help us."

Oh Lord. In my thirteen-year-old mind, I was thinking, "The world is coming to an end. I'm going to get thrown out of school." Later, I learned that I might have been leaping to conclusions—the situation was not quite that dire—but in my mind I understood that I needed to do something to help my parents because what I've always known is that we were in this together.

I thought of the sweet old woman who lived down the street from us. She was an Avon lady; she sold makeup door-to-door. She'd once asked me if I wanted to sell Avon products at my school. As payment, she'd offered me free lipsticks, eye shadow, and blush. It was a tempting offer, but I knew the nuns would never go for it. But that night, I had a different idea. I knew what I had to do. The next day I went to see the Avon lady.

"Remember how you asked if I wanted to sell Avon?" I

asked her. "I'd love to do it, but I want a better deal. It's got to be fifty-fifty." Where did I even come up with that? I must have seen it on a TV show. "Fifty-fifty" sounded like a grown-up business thing to say. And she actually agreed! She took me under her wing. I became her subagent. I started selling Avon to the girls at school and their moms. Word spread and everyone wanted my products. It was my first foray into viral marketing!

As soon as I had some money saved up, I planned to go to the nuns at school and start paying down my tuition. But I knew that my dad, the patriarch of our traditional Cuban family, would never be okay with this. He would not allow his daughter to pay her own tuition. So I went to the nuns and begged them not to tell my family. Instead, I asked them to write a letter to my parents saying that I had been awarded a partial scholarship. They agreed, and I brought the note home. My mother peered over my father's shoulder as he read it.

"What does it say?" she asked.

"Your daughter is a genius!" he said. "And you see? Jesus helped us after all."

It was my first lesson in financial empowerment. I had a problem, and I found a way to fix it by thinking entrepreneurially. Though I didn't have a name for it yet, I felt a surge of accomplishment, a sense of joy that came from doing something by myself, for myself, and it was something that helped my family. It was a seed of self-reliance that began to grow inside me, a glimpse of what was possible just by using the talents and resources I had at my disposal.

BOOTSTRAP YOUR WAY
TO SUCCESS

• • • •

I WANT YOU TO APPROPRIATE THE ATTITUDE AND VALUES OF immigrants—the bootstrap mentality—and put it to use in your own quest to become self-made. I promise you that in one generation, we can rewrite the economic stories of our families and create abundance. Here is a distillation of the immigrant approach:

- You live in the best place in the world for women and for business. Be grateful.
- Be willing to start at the bottom and work your way up.
- Give up your sense of entitlement. It's not serving you.
- You and your family are in it together. Work as a team.
- Start early and leave late, in everything you do.
- Be humble, ready, willing, and able to work and make money. Every road has a business lesson to teach you.
- Entrepreneurship takes passion and stamina. Remember, you are training to be an owner.
- Start with your own community. Look for people like you who are underserved and sell to them first.
- Get out of survival mode. Prepare for life's curveballs by working toward the goal of a secure future— today.

I want to help you channel the immigrant spirit, whatever your background, to achieve great things! I want to teach you how to think like an entrepreneur. I want to help you find the seed of self-reliance in yourself, wherever it may be, and nurture it. I want you to know the kind of peace and security that financial independence brings.

HOW TO PREPARE FOR THINGS BEYOND YOUR CONTROL

· · · ·

THE UNEXPECTED HAPPENS; IT'S A GIVEN. AND PARTICULARLY when it's something that's out of our hands, beyond our control, we feel vulnerable and afraid. Understandably, we get sad, we feel victimized, and we must mourn. However, it's important to remember how much of life is in our hands. We can choose not to be observers, watching life happen from a distance. We can be doers who create change in our lives and in the lives of those around us.

Living our best life is the only way to prepare ourselves for the unexpected. We must live the life we desire every day. But it doesn't just happen to us; we have to take action. We have to take steps (even baby steps) toward the life we want and the reality we dream about, because time is ticking away.

What is the one thing that you have wanted to do but you keep putting off? Going back to school? Time passes quickly; even if you start slowly—taking online courses or going to school at night—you will finish before you know it. Starting that diet? Brutal—I know from personal experience. Take it slow by losing half a pound a week—even a quarter of a pound! In a year, it will all add up. Start a business! Even if it's one hour a week, sell one item online, just start, and put that money away for your dreams. Acknowledging the things that you want and starting your journey toward them, even with the smallest actions, will put you in a place of power. And that's a much better place to be when the unexpected happens.

Begin by taking a personal inventory. Think about three things that you would like to act on this year. How far are you into the process? Don't beat yourself up if you are behind. Just think about the next small step you can take, and take it. Take it.

I AM SELF-MADE: Rupila Sethi

RUPILA SETHI GREW UP IN INDIA, ONE OF THREE children in a progressive, close-knit, Sikh family, and studied architecture at a prestigious university. When she was twenty-five, she decided she wanted to move to New York to pursue a graduate degree. Though her family believed strongly in the value of education, they initially objected because they wanted her to stay close to home and find a husband. Nevertheless, Rupila applied for and received an educational loan to study lighting design at Parsons School of Design. Her family, sad to see her move so far away, understood that this was an incredible opportunity that she couldn't turn down.

Rupila lived with an uncle, her only relative in New York, for a month while she started school. She soon found an affordable apartment in Queens that she shared with two roommates in order to save money and then took a job working for one of her professors to cover her expenses. She completed the master's in one year while working full-time. It was a challenging year, but Rupila took full advantage of every moment, learning to navigate New York City while making contacts in her industry.

After graduation, Rupila continued to work for her

professor at a design studio in downtown Manhattan and gained experience working on prestigious lighting projects for companies such as Tiffany, HBO, and LeSportsac. She also designed lighting for high-end residences in the United States and Kuwait, but something about the lighting industry made her feel stifled. There was very little artistry involved in her work, and Rupila craved a little creative freedom.

Soon after graduating, a friend from lighting school approached her about opening a restaurant in the West Village. Her family had been in the restaurant business back home. By now, Rupila had gotten married, and her husband was making a decent salary, so she decided to quit her job and focus on opening the restaurant. The restaurant became successful; it was in a hot neighborhood and got good reviews. Running a restaurant taught Rupila even more about New York. Until then, maybe she'd felt somewhat sheltered—following a path that was clearly laid out—but when she opened the restaurant, she saw what it was like to be in charge of her business. She learned how to deal with contractors, patrons, and staff; she learned her way around city regulations. She helped her friend run the restaurant for over two years, but the hours were long, and Rupila and her husband wanted to start a family. When her business partner offered to buy her out, Rupila accepted. At the time, she worried that she had wasted two years of her life, but in retrospect she realizes that those years taught her about running a business and helped her build connections. The experience wound up setting the foundation for what she does today.

Rupila wanted to get back into something architecture related, but in the meantime she worked a series of part-time jobs. One of them was working as a project manager at a construction company, and she loved the work she was doing. She quickly took on a larger role at the company, and one year later one of her bosses approached her about starting a construction company of their own. They decided to open Aerial Design and Build. Immediately, Aerial Design and Build had contracts with some high-profile companies and clients. Her partner had the technical knowledge, while Rupila was good at leveraging her contacts from lighting and the restaurant business to land contracts.

During the first four years that they were in business, Rupila had two children, and her partner moved to Greece. Jobs began to slow down, and they constantly worried about where the next big job would come from. They wanted to get some press attention to publicize what they were doing, in the hope of attracting more work. They heard about Count Me In, a nonprofit organization that helps women-owned businesses by providing free business coaching, financial training, and publicity opportunities. Rupila and her partner took time out of the day-to-day to apply for the Count Me In program—a competitive process—and were accepted. With the mentorship and the press that the competition provided, their business once again took off. They had the foresight to be thinking of the future of their business, the next hill to climb, instead of being consumed by the present. Five years later, Aerial Design and Build now has annual revenue of over seven million dollars.

make fear and failure your best friends.

BEFORE I GET UP ONSTAGE TO SPEAK AT MY EVENTS, I show a three-minute video of my accomplishments so that people in the audience know who I am and why I am standing there in front of them. That video is purposely impressive; in the business, it's called a sizzle reel. Even I'm impressed when I watch it; I fall for my own story. But when I take the stage, the first thing I tell the audience is that if I were to show my failure reel, it would be three times as long as my sizzle reel. And it would make you cry.

The two-headed demon of fear and failure is hands down the biggest obstacle to overcome on our self-made journey.

Fear and failure are always present in our lives. And they go together, hand in hand. First, we have to accept that they are inevitable. Then we have to learn to confront them. At first you will be afraid of everything. Then you'll take a chance and you'll be afraid of failing—and you will fail, trust me! When you do, you'll think the world is coming to an end, but here you have to trust me again: It isn't.

People have said to me, "Of course you've accomplished all that you have. You're fearless!" And I laugh because it's so far from the truth. But years ago, I decided that I had to make fear and failure my best friends, my guiding light. They were showing up so often in my life that I had to learn to accept them and pay attention to what they were trying to tell me.

Even today, fear can make me pass on a great opportunity, and failure is still very painful for me. I don't take it lightly; sometimes I don't get out of bed for days after a major set-back. But when the two-headed demon shows up, I trust that she is there to tell me something, to point me in the direction of something I wouldn't have recognized otherwise. I've learned that she deserves my respect. I say hello and pay attention to what she's telling me. Fear is showing me that there is something I must do even if it scares me, and failure is showing me that I missed a piece of the puzzle that I need to see in order to get it right the next time. My greatest successes have often come quick on the heels of my worst failures. (The same is true, by the way, for jealousy. I pay attention. I ask myself what it is about this person I am coveting. How can I acquire it? How can I learn from it?)

I had to learn this behavior, because in my culture Latinas

are raised in a fear cloud. I've observed that this is true for other multicultural women too. Failure is a stigma. But failure is built into the American experience. Fear shows up—do it anyway. That's the American way. And there's something to be learned from Silicon Valley, where failure is celebrated as a stop on the road to success.

I've also had to learn that fear is not a fact; it's just a feeling. It's something you have to work through. Failure, on the other hand, has to be mourned before you can move on. *¡Adelante!* Let's go! Do it. Don't think; just do it. In spite of fear and failure, let your actions lead the way, and your feelings will follow.

CONFRONTING MY FEARS

· · · ·

BETWEEN THE AGES OF FIVE AND TEN, I DEVELOPED ALL KINDS of fear-based phobias. I was afraid of walking in the snow. I was afraid of noises. I was afraid of rocks. I bit my nails. I was consumed by fear and anxiety. I would cry all the time. Yet I was my parents' translator, a decision maker in the family, their rock. I now see that my phobias were the one place I got to be a kid. They got me attention; they got me my parents' care and concern.

In sixth grade, things had gotten really bad. I was being bullied by a girl in school, and I was miserable. I could tell that this girl sensed my fear and that was why she was picking on me. I realized that my only choice was to stand up to her.

So one day I yelled at her, and then I actually pushed her into a trash can! I'm almost embarrassed to admit that part of the story, and—don't get me wrong—I'm not recommending that you push someone into a trash can to overcome your fears. But she never bothered me again.

What I want you to understand is that it is possible to transform your fear in a snap. As I said, fear is a feeling, not a fact. If someone or something in your life is hurting you, you have the strength and the ability to put a stop to it and to make a change. I know this because I did it. My mother calls it my "great metamorphosis." She actually started calling me ET after it happened, because she said that a brave extraterrestrial must have taken over her daughter's body!

Banishing my childhood fears didn't mean that fear was gone from my life. Years later, in my thirties, some of my phobias returned. Suddenly I became afraid of heights. I knew what I had to do. The brave version of me took skydiving classes and jumped out of a plane; I have the video to prove it! You don't necessarily have to jump out of a plane to confront your fears, but you get the idea. I was never afraid of heights again!

WHEN FEAR TAKES YOU
TO A HIGHER PLACE

· · · ·

I LOVE THESE LINES FROM THE POET RILKE: "THE FUTURE EN-ters into us . . . in order to transform itself in us long before it happens." They remind me of this: Good things can happen, even if we can't see them yet.

In 2007, I sold a show that I was really excited about to NBC; it was, to my mind, a groundbreaking reality series about female empowerment. I envisioned a robust online component that would allow fans to track the progress of contestants via social media. Then the recession hit in 2008, and advertiser money got tight, and the networks were contracting. My show was moved off the schedule indefinitely. It was a huge disappointment to me.

Around this time, Ben Silverman, the then co-chairman of NBC, invited me to be on the first season of *The Celebrity Apprentice*. The show was totally new at the time, and he had to explain the whole concept behind it. He thought it was important to have an empowered Latina who could really hold her own on the show. Immediately, fear rose up in me. "I'm not a celebrity," I thought. "Why would they want me on a show called *The* Celebrity *Apprentice*?" I was a behind-the-scenes person. I thought to myself, "You are not one of them. You're not on-air talent." So I said to him, "Are you kidding? I'm not a celebrity."

Silverman's response: "Why don't you just thank me for offering you millions of dollars of free marketing and publicity for your business? By the end of the show, you will be a celebrity." So I pushed through my fear, accepted his offer, and thanked him profusely.

Appearing on *The Celebrity Apprentice* turned out to be one of the greatest experiences of my life. I was sequestered for six weeks with a group of people who were brilliant in completely different ways. The cast included Gene Simmons from Kiss (one of the smartest people I would meet in my life), the boxer Lennox Lewis, the actress Marilu Henner (who, I learned, has a savant-like memory), the perfect-10 gymnast Nadia Comaneci, the British journalist Piers Morgan, and the woman who set the bar for all the notorious reality show villainesses who followed, Omarosa, who actually is very smart and competent. And of course, there was the ultimate reality show ringleader Donald Trump—who was, at the time, just a successful businessman, not yet a politician. All in all, a fascinating group.

I spent a lot of time with Gene Simmons, who, when you get past the images of him in his crazy face paint and platform boots, is extremely perceptive and thoughtful. His observations and insights constantly blew my mind. Simmons and I were on the same team, and at one point he actually allowed himself to be fired from the show to save me. By then, we had bonded, and before he left the show, I called to thank him.

"Gene, I don't even know what to say. You took a bullet for me."

"You deserve it, Galán," he said. "But can I give you one piece of advice? Why do I feel like you're an immigrant climbing a mountain in the hardest possible way? You work hard but not smart. You don't let yourself enjoy what you're doing. It's almost like you don't enjoy the journey if it's not hard. Don't you know that you don't need to do that anymore? Don't you know that you are already successful, that you have an incredible Rolodex at this point? Why aren't you doing something bigger with your life? I feel like you are meant for something greater. Why don't you take some time off and come up with a bigger mission for your life?"

I felt as if I couldn't breathe. At that moment, I couldn't take in that he was actually giving me a compliment. Instead, what he said cut me to the bone.

The show ended, I returned home, and I was again in a panic about my business because the economy was now in a free fall. Brian said to me, "Nely, what *are* you so afraid of? Let me ask you something: What would you want to do today if you found out you only had a year to live?"

I knew the answer right away. "I would finish school. I'd go back and get my degree." I knew I'd sacrificed and missed out, working during the years I should have been in college, getting an education. I had a lot of life experience I wanted to process too; I wanted to study psychology.

"Then go do it!" he said. So I did. I took a four-year sabbatical from my TV business. At first, I had mild panic attacks every day. I felt guilty, irresponsible, and lazy. My fearful, negative inner voice said, "Who do you think you are?" And the shock in my friends' and family's faces when I told them corroborated my own negative thinking. But I could feel that my fear was guiding me to a higher place, so I stuck it out.

During my first month in school, a professor read one of my papers and said, "What is this? You write like a rapper." I had worked in media my whole life, and the way I wrote was shaped by the way you talk to people in the entertainment business when you're trying to sell them something in a hurry.

"You need to learn to write all over again. Here's a copy of *The Elements of Style* by Strunk and White, the classic book on English syntax and grammar. Learn how to write, redo your paper, and hand it in again."

I went home and told Brian what my professor said. He said, "Wow, the professor actually said that to you? I think I'd give up if somebody said that to me."

"No, I'm going to a higher place," I said. "I have to humble myself and go backward in order to move forward." At that moment, something clicked. I suddenly understood what Gene Simmons had been telling me: I needed to take the time to prepare myself for my next stage of growth. I needed to aim higher. I knew then that my decision to go back to school had been the right one. I needed to take a break and look at everything I'd done in my life, analyze it, see where the gaps in my education were, and fill them so I could take myself to a higher place.

Sometimes, fear helps move you from where you are to where you need to be. It is an alert that you're leaving your comfort zone. I had gotten by on chutzpah all my life, but I had missed some important milestones, and my fear was showing me that I had to go back and do the work.

I was setting the stage for the next chapter in my journey. My studies in psychology gave me the tools and insight to examine and understand my personal battles as an immigrant and my journey as a woman, a Latina, and a self-made entrepreneur. Suddenly the puzzle revealed itself. If the economy had not crashed, if my show had not been taken away from me, if I had not agreed to go on *The Celebrity Appren-*

tice, I would not have gone back to school to study psychology, and I wouldn't have had the realization that my ideas about female empowerment were bigger than a TV show. Writing my thesis and dissertation about the struggles of women and Latinas became the foundation for the Self-Made movement, which led to touring the country to spread my message and eventually to writing this book.

Pushing through fear is never easy, but you learn from it and you grow. And ultimately, it changes you. Don't ever let fear stop you. Ever. Think of me as your skydiving instructor. I'm not going to push you out of the plane, but I'm going to teach you how to check your parachute, and your backup parachute, and I'm going to show you how to land.

sometimes when you lose, you win

I couldn't help getting in the shoes of Miss Colombia at the 2015 Miss Universe pageant. I felt for her. She had just won Miss Universe, and then, just a few moments later—oops! it was a mistake!—she lost to Miss Philippines, and the crown was abruptly taken off her head. At first glance, I am sure it was a devastating and humiliating moment for her.

But, did she really lose? First of all, the publicity she will get from this mistake will kick-start her career. Sometimes a loss can point the way toward a bigger idea, a bigger mission. Sometimes a loss saves you from a big mistake. Sometimes a loss opens the door to something that is better for you, more aligned with your true self, and the better path in the end.

At this moment in time, is being Miss Universe the aspiration it once was, or is the new goal to be Ms. Mogul? I recently read a great article in *More* magazine titled "Smart Is the New Beautiful." I think Miss Colombia will realize this, if she hasn't already. I think she will do better by having lost the crown. The world is hers, and she is free to explore it, out of the box of her title or her beauty. I hope she will cultivate a new version—a deeper and better version—of herself.

choose yourself first.

HERE IS A VARIATION ON THE PRINCE CHARMING RESCUE fantasy. I call it the "chosen" fantasy. It's a magical transformation that occurs just by being in the right place at the right time. It involves being plucked from obscurity, chosen by luck or circumstance to ascend to instant happiness, fame, or success. It goes like this: Someone with the power to make things happen is going to see you—the real you, the version of yourself that you aspire to, that you keep hidden down deep inside—and that person is going to choose you and deliver you to the self you were meant to be. It's a fantasy that trades on those fairy-tale stories about the girl who gets discovered at the mall and becomes a famous model, or the charming delivery guy who one day makes a delivery to a casting agent . . . Maybe your version is closer to this: One day, at work, you're going to speak up in a meeting, and the big boss is going to recognize how brilliant you truly are. Suddenly, he sees you in a whole, new light—*you are executive material!*— and he puts you on a career fast track. Or maybe your chosen fantasy goes like this: You like to bake, so you bake your famous brownies for the school bake sale. Unbeknownst to you, one of the other parents is a wealthy venture capitalist. She tastes your creation and is blown away and offers to back you and turn your product into a successful brand!

Most of us would never admit it, but we secretly hope that we'll be chosen. We think, "If I work hard and do all of the right things, someone will notice me and I will finally be rewarded." But the truth is to be chosen, *you have to choose yourself first*. You can't sit around waiting for someone else to make success happen for you. *You* have to be the one to make it happen, and that starts with recognizing your gifts and your strengths. It means having a goal and honoring that goal and stating your intention to realize that goal. Don't wait for magic to happen. Make it happen. *Choose yourself first!*

So what exactly do I mean by choose yourself? By way of explanation, I'll tell you a story from my own career. When I was thirty-five, I was called by an executive at Sony who was recruiting for the position of president of the Spanish-language U.S.-based TV network Telemundo. He wanted to meet with me about the job. President! The first Latina network president! That was the job I'd dreamed about since I was a girl. On the wall of my teenage bedroom, I had taped up pictures from *Vanity Fair* of Sherry Lansing, my idol—the first female president of a movie studio, 20th Century Fox. While I was qualified for the Telemundo position, I was also an outsider. I had been running my own TV production company; I was an independent contractor, providing TV content to networks. I had the networks as my clients, but I was not one of the guys in the corporate club.

During our interview, he said rather bluntly, "You seem like a bit of a rogue entrepreneur to me, and this is a very corporate job." My heart stopped. He was a brilliant exec who would go on to great accomplishments in Hollywood, and I appreciated his honesty. I understood that he was saying that he saw me as more of a nonconformist who would go her own way, rather than someone who put the needs of the corporation first. In hindsight, he was probably onto something (I couldn't hide my entrepreneurial spirit!), but I'd already decided that I wanted that job; it was the job for me. Once he spoke those words, I felt as if I'd blown it.

I knew I had to do something drastic to erase this notion in his mind and convince him that I was the ideal candidate for the job, so I went back to my office and got to work producing a tape of what I thought Telemundo should look like. I hired a design team to create a look for the network. I pulled video that was representative of the campaign I envisioned, with the message that being Latino in the United States is the best of both worlds. I hired editors and worked with them for a week. I paid for it with my own money. I sent the tape to the executive. It was the kind of tape someone would make who was already running the company. That tape got me the job.

I'd made a conscious decision to choose myself, trusting that the rest of the world would follow.

How had I known what to do? I'd had a lot of practice choosing myself, and that's what I want you to do: Identify your goal, who you want to be—that person who you dream will be "discovered"—and practice choosing yourself until you can comfortably inhabit that role. Do what it takes to convince yourself—take real action, educate yourself, create the kinds of things that would be expected of you in that role. It won't feel comfortable at first; sometimes it's terrifying. But you've got to make it a reflex. It's like a muscle that you have to exercise until it becomes strong.

When did I first begin to cultivate this instinct? During my sophomore year of high school, one of the nuns—my favorite nun!—accused me of plagiarism. I'd written a short story about the death of an old woman in a Cuban fishing village. I guess it was pretty good, because the nun thought I'd ripped off Ernest Hemingway. I was suspended from school for three days and sent home. When I tried to explain things to my parents, they took the nun's side. As immigrants, they were always afraid; everything brought shame. I understand it now, but at the time I was furious! They told me, "You need to go back and apologize to your teacher." I was outraged! I hadn't done anything wrong, but they wouldn't listen to me.

I know now that anger can be a very powerful tool if you harness it properly. It can motivate you to do something grand, to beat the system. I was angry with my parents for not supporting me. I was angry at the nun for thinking that a studious Goody Two-Shoes like me would ever dream of plagiarizing. And I found a way to channel that anger. During my suspension, I sat in the attic of our house and wrote an essay: "Why You Should Never Send Your Daughter to an All-Girls Catholic School." I sent it to *Seventeen* magazine, my favorite.

Three days later, I went back to school, and the nun called me into her office. "I am so sorry, Nely," she said. "Something about your story reminded me of a Hemingway story, but I was wrong. I applaud you for writing such a good story. I just can't believe you wrote something this serious at fifteen."

"I guess I have deep thoughts for a teenager," I replied. She gave me an A plus on the assignment.

A few months passed, and things blew over at school. Then, one day, I got a letter from someone named Lori, an editorial assistant, on *Seventeen* letterhead: "Congratulations! We've chosen your article to be published in *Seventeen*. Enclosed is a $100 check." Can you imagine being a teenager and getting that letter? I was a Catholic schoolgirl, so of course I felt as if God were giving me a sign. I felt as if I had been chosen, but really, when I wrote and sent that essay, I was choosing myself.

When the article was published, I panicked, and again the nuns freaked out. A teenage girl writing that story today might be the next Lena Dunham, but back then nuns had no sense of humor. The article caused a sensation, and I was offered a guest editorship at *Seventeen*. At this point, I also had enough credits to graduate early from high school. So I did, and I began commuting from New Jersey into Manhattan for a yearlong internship. (And in case you're wondering, I took a sales job at the Limited, a clothing store, to pay my own way, because the internship at the magazine was unpaid.)

The moral of the story wasn't lost on me: When you take action and choose yourself, there's the possibility something will happen. If you take no action, I can guarantee you nothing will happen.

Listen, there have been many times in my life when I took action and things didn't work out so well. But it's okay if it doesn't work out every time. Think of it as practice. The point is to get into the habit of choosing yourself until it becomes second nature. In my case, maybe it was just beginner's luck. But it allowed me to experience the thrill of what choosing yourself, and being rewarded for it, can feel like. I actually thought to myself, "Oh my God. I am meant to do great things."

I often meet women at my events who say things like "I like to cook" instead of "I am a chef," or "I help organize my friends' closets" instead of "I am a stylist." I tell them, "Ladies, if you want people to see you as you are, you have to declare yourself! This is a country that likes people who are loud and who stand up for what they believe in. We like courage. This is probably the only country in the world that rewards boldness. So take action. Speak up. Be bold. Declare yourself. Say, 'I drive for Uber and I am self-made.' Say, 'I own an online store and I am self-made.'" Choose yourself. And when you do, people will notice you, and they will choose you over and over again.

SELF
MADE

CHOOSE YOURSELF.
AND WHEN YOU DO,
PEOPLE WILL
NOTICE YOU,
AND THEY WILL
CHOOSE YOU
OVER AND OVER
AGAIN.

INVEST IN YOURSELF

· · · ·

I BELIEVE YOU HAVE TO KILL PARTS OF YOURSELF FOR OTHER parts to be reborn. That negative voice inside your head that tells you, *Who do you think you are?* She's got to go in order for you to choose yourself. How do you make her go away? How do you get rid of the baggage and the resentments that hold you back and weigh you down so the better, stronger, forward-facing parts of you can take flight? It takes work—a lot of work. Inner work. Choosing yourself involves introspection.

During the four years I went back to school, there were many deaths for me, anger I had to let go of, things I had to make peace with. Therapy helped with that—a lot. But writing also helped. I've had a weekly practice of writing for years. I've kept a diary since I was seven years old. Every week I write in my diary the things I am grateful for, my accomplishments for the week, the things I still need to work on. And things come up; you start to see themes. Some negative, some positive. Those are the things you have to decide to kill or to cultivate. Choosing yourself is true self-help, DIY therapy. And along the way, you may also need or want to get professional help. I want you to see that as an investment in yourself.

If you don't feel comfortable with therapy, get a life coach. If you don't feel that that's your style, go to a spiritual teacher—a priest, a pastor, a nun, a rabbi, whoever fills that role in your life. There's plenty of help out there; no one should feel she has to go it alone.

There is much to be learned from paying attention to yourself. Everything you do, every choice you've made or will make, is important, because *you* are important. There is no narcissism or grandiosity in this. It's about putting yourself in the mindset that your actions count, that your decisions have implications, and that you have chosen yourself and put your faith in your own ability to succeed. Your biggest investment is staring at you in the mirror. When you commit to becoming self-made, what you are investing in, ultimately, is yourself.

WHO'S ON YOUR TEAM?

. . . .

I LIKE TO REMIND PEOPLE THAT KOBE BRYANT HAS TWENTY COACHES. Are you less important than Kobe Bryant?

Investing in yourself means building a team of people who can teach you skills you don't know, complement skills you have, and support you in many ways, including emotionally. Take classes or hire a tutor or, better yet, barter your skills for someone else's. Maybe you're embarrassed that you don't know your way around technology or social media. You're not alone; the digital world is moving very fast. I know billionaires who have hired tutors to coach them about the Internet. I know billionaires who have studied accounting and legal matters—the meat-and-potatoes stuff of businesses—because they want to know enough to question the people who work for them.

When I was running a little TV station, I realized I didn't have the preparation I needed, particularly in math. I hated math. So I put an ad in the paper because that's how I thought you did it, and I got a response from a lady named Ophelia. Ophelia! I'll never forget her. Ophelia became my math tutor. She'd come to the office three times a week and teach me the math of my business. She loved math so much that she flipped the switch in my head and made me love math. Now I can teach math to anyone. I actually love accounting, love balancing the books.

If you don't have the money or the time for a tutor, take a class. There are free night school classes. There are online courses on YouTube. Visit the Khan Academy online, an incredible resource for math, economics, finance, and computer science.

Join a young entrepreneurs club, like Entrepreneurs' Organization (eonetwork.org), or become a member of your local chamber of commerce, where you'll find people ready and willing to help you with your business. Chambers of commerce offer training, information, and networking events where you'll meet other entrepreneurs just like you. At work, put yourself up for the Latino or African American or Asian association in your company. Or join a professional organization or collective.

The point is to create a community of coaches, a great talented pool of resources you can draw on. You don't have to do this alone. At every step, you have an ally to help you along the way.

I AM SELF-MADE: Miracle Wanzo

MIRACLE WANZO LOVED FASHION BUT PURSUED a degree in business because she thought it was more practical. After college, she followed a traditional path and took a job working for a pharmaceutical company. Miracle was happy with her company and had begun to move up the ladder. After she had her first child, she realized that the life she had thought she wanted didn't afford her enough time with her family. Working from home and telecommuting weren't options, and the long hours and commute were becoming huge sources of stress. She realized that she wanted to leave the corporate world and work for herself; she wanted to become self-made.

In the late 1990s, Miracle recognized that there was a huge opportunity for her in e-commerce. The Internet was relatively new, and there weren't many people with serious e-retail businesses to learn from, so she started researching apparel suppliers online and making connections in SCORE, the consulting arm of the Small Business Administration (SBA), looking for consultants with connections to the fashion industry. After a few months, she had made enough contacts and invested in a diverse inventory; she then began selling discounted branded and designer apparel on eBay. She kept her job with the pharmaceutical company, but at the same time she committed to making her online business work. In about a year and a half, her eBay business was strong enough that she felt secure in leaving her corporate job.

In time, Miracle decided to shift gears. She wanted more control over her inventory, and with discounted apparel she never knew what colors and sizes she would get in her shipments. She moved the majority of her business off eBay and started an online business that sold lingerie, hipundies.com. A friend of hers ran a successful online shop that sold swimsuits, and Miracle recognized that her business would likely follow a similar trajectory. She could benefit from her friend's experience. Miracle immediately took whatever orders she could from intimate manufacturers who would fill small orders, put inventory up on her site, and began taking and filling orders. In that way, hipundies.com had immediate profits.

At the time, there was little competition in lingerie e-commerce. Miracle learned how to run the business while that limited inventory sold, and she also used that time to approach larger brands, pointing them to her functioning site to illustrate how she could market and sell inventory. As her selection grew, so did her profits, but as e-commerce became more popular, these brands were beginning to sell directly to consumers online. She knew it was only a matter of time before she would have to compete with brand-specific websites, so Miracle took a risk and invested the earnings from hipundies. com into manufacturing her own lingerie line under the

Hip Undies brand name both domestically and abroad. She wanted to be able to provide a unique product and control the quantity and price. Miracle relied heavily on the growing online community for advice. She joined organizations such as Count Me In, Facebook groups, eCommerceFuel, and the Dynamite Circle—gated online communities where members must meet an online revenue threshold to join. These fellow e-retailers provided Miracle with advice and support.

Miracle, a single mother of four, employs her children in her business, showing them the value of being self-made. She was always looking toward the future, acquiring new knowledge and investing the money she made back into her business, making it more efficient and profitable. She immersed herself in the community around her and online, learning every aspect of her business and marrying her passion and her skills to create a successful, dynamic company. She chose herself over and over again.

ACT "AS IF"

· · · ·

WHEN I TELL WOMEN MY CRAZY STORIES ABOUT CHOOSING MY-self, they always ask, "But how did you do it? How did you have the guts?" I'll tell you a secret: I couldn't have done these things just by being myself. "Just be yourself" is not the way to go in professional situations. When I need an extra boost of confidence, I have this little trick: I channel the confidence and energy of people I admire, people I think of as brave and empowered. I call this "acting as if." This is not about being "fake"; it's more like a shortcut to confidence when you're feeling intimidated. And I promise, "acting as if" works! I learned this trick early in my career when I was feeling intimidated working around successful people.

When I needed to be brave, I would summon the energy and authority and polish of some of my former bosses. At *Seventeen,* I worked with Andrea Robinson, a beauty editor who later went on to run Revlon and L'Oréal. She was beautiful and supercompetent and empowered. I later worked for the TV producer Aida Barrera, who was very decisive and tough. In the early 1980s, I worked for the legendary Monique Pillard, who ran Elite Model Management and managed the careers of Iman, Christie Brinkley, Kim Alexis, and other supermodels. Monique was like a tough but loving mom who could make grown men cry with her negotiating techniques. Often I was scared to death underneath it all, but when I had to bring it, I would channel these women I admired and bring them with me into a big meeting, interview, or presentation. I'd ask myself, "What would Monique or Andrea or Aida do?" And then I would go and do it. As my career progressed, I added many other mentors, male and female, to my roster. I cherry-picked from their attitudes, their one-liners, and their deal-making skills.

When you learn from the best and model yourself after

them, somehow along the way you actually find your own unique voice, your own strength, and a style that sounds authentically like you. When I was a contestant on *The Celebrity Apprentice,* I had more than a few tough arguments with Donald Trump in the boardroom. Women would write to me and ask, "How do you have the guts to speak to Trump that way, especially as a Latina?" By then, I had found a powerful and authentic voice of my own. I was no longer the little girl from Cuba who would cry when teachers or kids said something that hurt her feelings. Today I feel so proud when women I have mentored and worked with tell me, "When I get stuck, I ask myself, 'What would Nely do in this situation?' and I act as if I'm you!" This brings me such joy because I know that these women are on their way to empowerment. Trust me, the trick works.

HIRE A PROFESSIONAL

· · · ·

WE ALL DEAL WITH INSECURITIES. WHEN I WAS MADE PRESIDENT of Telemundo, I was concerned—not about the work, the stress, or the fact that I had to manage so many people, but about my lack of style. In those days, I had no idea how to dress fashionably *and* professionally, and people sometimes got the wrong idea about me. Who could help me? Why not a *Vogue* fashion editor? I didn't know if an editor would do such a thing, but I thought there was no harm in asking.

I was lucky; from my days at *Seventeen,* I'd made friends

in the fashion business. Through them, I found a young African American woman who'd worked as an editor at *Vogue*. She was up for the challenge. I used to wear loud clothes with a lot of bedazzling and tchotchkes on them. More *cuchifrito* than presidential. She convinced me that my clothes should be quiet, because I was loud enough. She created a gorgeous, sophisticated palette and came up with my new look. She shopped for me and constructed a book with snapshots of outfits matched to accessories for every day of the week. Suddenly a burden was lifted from my shoulders. I learned the art of dressing and followed my little look book until I no longer needed it. Most important, I no longer had to worry about whether I was dressed appropriately. I knew I looked great. I was free to focus entirely on my job. And it ended up being cheaper to hire her than to get my clothes from a store because she got me my entire wardrobe at wholesale prices!

Most department stores now have a personal shopping department where a professional shopper can help you improve your wardrobe for free as long as you buy the clothes there. You don't always need an in with a *Vogue* editor, but you do need to search out the resources that are available to you and take advantage of them. You're worth it.

EXERCISE:

Acting As If

I call this process of channeling others you admire "acting as if." Here are some questions to ask yourself in order to begin channeling the energy and confidence of your mentors:

o   Whom do you admire? (It can be people you know, celebrities, or people you've admired from afar.)

o   Who are the five women or men in your life with qualities you would most like to emulate and why?

o   Who is the bravest person you know?

o   Who speaks to people in a respectful but powerful way?

o   How can you model yourself after these empowered people?

Make yourself a binder—a look book—and fill it with images of the woman you want to be. Tear pictures out of magazines; jot down notes of what you like about the images. What would that woman look like, and how would she sound? How would she exercise

command a room? Now circle the words or phrases that appear again and again. That repetition is your thread. A thread tells you what is missing in your life. Write down your thread.

Who on the list epitomizes this trait? Turn this person or these people into your dream mentor. Whenever you get stuck, ask yourself, what would they do? Would they be embarrassed to ask to be paid for a service? How would they dress for a presentation? Think of questions that you'd like to ask your dream mentor. Try to imagine the ways he or she would answer those questions.

I AM SELF-MADE: Princess Jenkins

PRINCESS JENKINS GREW UP A TOMBOY IN THE Bronx with a passion for fabric and design. As a young girl, she would sit on her stoop and sketch clothing while the other children played. Eventually, she started to re-design her wardrobe using embroidery and crocheting to make her clothes unique. At age thirteen, she went to the Dover Theater to see the film *Mahogany*. Diana Ross plays an aspiring designer who struggles to learn the fashion business and ultimately achieves fame. From that moment on, Princess knew that she wanted to be a fashion designer. She shed her tomboy persona and fashioned herself after Mahogany, the Diana Ross char-acter. She acted as if.

In high school, Princess took advantage of an execu-tive internship program sponsored by the New York City Board of Education; in it, seniors were selected to forgo their regular classes and get on-the-job experience for four months. Princess applied and requested an intern-ship with a designer. The program tried to place her in an internship with a dance studio—Princess was also an ac-complished dancer—but she persevered. Channeling *Mahogany*, Princess told the organization that she was exclusively interested in interning in the fashion industry.

Eventually, she was placed in an internship with Vera Maxwell, a sportswear designer. Princess worked at Vera's studio for over three years, starting as an errand girl. She worked for free five days a week, was always on time, made sure she kept the receipts for everything she picked up, and built trust with the people in the studio. Vera eventually moved Princess to a paid position in her showroom, putting her in charge of accessories for all fashion shows. During this time, Princess was exposed to a wide variety of people in the fashion industry, and she parlayed those connections into a career.

Princess is now the president of the Brownstone, a women's clothing boutique in Harlem that has been featured on *Good Day New York* and *Good Morning America*. With her success as a business owner, she decided to fulfill another mission that was important to her. In 1998, Princess Jenkins founded Women in the Black, a Harlem-based entrepreneurial organization created for the purpose of educating, training, and supporting women who have started their own businesses. She has helped counsel, promote, and provide assistance to over twenty-five hundred entrepreneurial women since the Brownstone opened.

LEAVING HOME

· · · ·

WHEN I WAS SEVENTEEN, AS MY *SEVENTEEN* MAGAZINE INTERN-ship was coming to a close, I was preparing to start college. Unexpectedly, I was contacted by the producer Aida Barrera, who'd been made aware of my work at the magazine. She was launching a TV show called *Checking It Out* that was like a teenage version of *60 Minutes*. She offered me a job as a researcher. There was one problem (aside from the fact that I was supposed to be headed to college): The show was based in Austin, Texas. I had a glimpse of my future in the TV business and in Aida, who was a real role model. I was going no matter what! When I told my mother, she said, "Niña, Dios mio, no! I am not letting you go to Texas! You're seventeen years old!" But I saw it as an opportunity I couldn't let pass me by.

"Mom, I'm almost eighteen," I said, "and if you don't let me go, I'm going to run away."

My mother cried hysterically the day I left. I packed up my little orange Chevy Chevette and drove halfway across the country by myself. Let me explain something: Latinas don't leave home like that. I was putting myself first, putting my needs before the needs of the family, or so it seemed. I knew that my destiny was not in Teaneck, New Jersey. That was not the life I wanted. I knew I had to make a radical change.

"I will never forgive you for leaving me," my mother told me. God, that was tough to hear. I was my mother's translator, her confidante, and her friend. Even knowing all that, I don't think I could fully appreciate how devastating this was for her until I had a child of my own.

Sometimes I wonder, what would my life look like if I had not left Teaneck? Today my mother will admit that although it was terribly difficult for her to accept, I made the right choice. She'd wanted me to stay because she was afraid. But after I left, she started to think about going back to school and learning to drive, and eventually she did both. What might have seemed like a selfish act of self-determination, leaving my parents and home behind to strike out on my own, was in fact something that turned out to be for the greater good of my family. Today, my parents are living an incredible life in retirement because I left Teaneck for that TV job. So let me ask you this: Was I really being selfish? As they tell you on airplanes, you have to put the oxygen mask on yourself first. In order to be your best for others—your parents, your kids, your partner—you have to choose yourself and take care of yourself first.

So here's what I want you to do: Put yourself out there. Write letters to people you want to meet. Blog, write articles online, have a voice, express yourself. Declare your intentions. Tell the world who you are. Take risks, knowing they won't all work out, but do it because courage is a practice you need to get comfortable with. Don't sit around waiting for great things to happen to you. Choose yourself first and be a fighter! Show others that you are worth choosing.

I AM

. . . .

CHOOSING YOURSELF IS ABOUT IDENTITY. YOU HAVE TO KNOW who you are before others can see you completely.

When I went back to school to study psychology, we were given an assignment to write a poem about ourselves called "I Am." Here's what I wrote:

I am in the hallway between lives,
In the past,
I never watched others do, but did what others
    watched.
I didn't let inevitable change rule my life,
    but rather, created change that affected time.
Sometimes when I won, I lost. Sometimes when
    I lost, I won.
I told stories that only I could tell and
    Made fear and failure my best friends.
I am a Swan
    With nothing to prove, I burned my résumé.
Becoming
    has taken a long time.
But now, finally,
I am Nely and I am self-made.

I have one more exercise to ask of you. Write your own poem that begins with "I am . . ." and ends with who you are and your declaration of being self-made. Then share it with us at becomingSELFMADE.com. We can't wait to read about your journey.

power is taken, not given.

L IFE IS A PUZZLE THAT REVEALS ITSELF SLOWLY. WE arrive at a fork in the road, a place where going left or right could change the entire trajectory of our story. Over time, if we're lucky, we will get to look back at these defining moments as the events that made us who we are and showed us who we could be. When I think about the stepping-stone moments in my own life, there's the Avon lady story, which was my first taste of self-sufficiency; the time I was accused of plagiarism, which taught me the value of speaking out on my own behalf; and the first time I understood what it meant to have an ownership stake in my own career.

When I was twenty-two years old, I became the manager of a small Spanish-language TV station, WNJU, which was based in Teterboro, New Jersey, and served ten million Latinos in the greater New York metropolitan area. I had been working in television for five years, in jobs in various cities across the country, and I had finally made my way to a job that I loved. I'd always been the small fish in a big pond, and now I was the big fish in a small pond. That job became my everything. It was action-packed. I felt as if I was learning and growing every day. I was creating programming for my community. I would meet with advertisers, and I'd make it up as I went along, which I found to be really exciting. I was learning how to run a business on someone else's dime. The New York *Daily News* had even published a story about the station, which it called "a gem of the city," and referred to me as its "Cuban missile" station manager—the youngest in the country. Even though I worked twenty-four hours a day and had no life, I felt that I had died and gone to heaven because I loved my job so much.

One morning, three years into the job, I came to work to find the company's white-haired attorney sitting in front of my office. That morning's *telenovela* played silently on the monitors. I wondered what I had done wrong. He greeted me and escorted me into my office, closed the door, and happily announced, "We sold the station to an insurance company. A very big deal. Isn't that great?" He kept talking, but I zoned out.

I was speechless, thinking, "Great for me? How?" I rushed to the bathroom and threw up. I was filled with anxiety. All I

POWER IS TAKEN, NOT GIVEN

could think was, "What will happen to me? I'm going to lose my job!"

Quickly, my fear turned into anger. How could my boss have sold the company without even telling me? I was part of the team! I WAS the company!

Impulsively, I stormed out of the building, got into my car, and, crying the whole way, drove over the George Washington Bridge into Manhattan, to the Park Avenue headquarters, to confront my boss. I took the elevator up fourteen floors, pushed past his assistant, and stormed into his office. I found my scary boss on the phone, joyfully regaling the person on the other end about the sale. I blurted out, "How could you do this to me? Why didn't you tell me?" And then I got choked up and started to cry. Bad move.

He raised his hand, palm toward my face—a stop sign—to silence me. "Young lady," he said, "those are our chips. You want to play? Go get your own chips."

I was devastated. In that moment, I hated him. "What a jerk," I thought as I walked out, feeling humiliated, like a stupid little girl. "Go get your own chips"? I sacrificed three years of my life for this job, no dates, no movie nights . . . I was a glorified twenty-four-hour-a-day worker bee.

Once I calmed down, I realized that this guy had just done me a huge favor. He had taught me an important lesson: Until that moment, I had been tied to the idea that I had to be somebody's employee. But in a split second, a light was turned on, and I realized that I had to think bigger. *I needed to think like an owner.*

For three years, I had been perfectly content to slave away

and run this business for my boss. In my wildest imagination, I had never thought that my dream job could suddenly disappear or that my boss wouldn't take care of me. I decided that I never wanted to have something I'd worked so hard for taken away from me again. I would never let anything like this happen to me again. I decided then and there to be my own boss and start my own business. "Go get your own chips!" would become my rallying cry.

LOWER YOUR OVERHEAD, PART I

. . . .

ONCE I GOT OVER THE SHOCK OF LOSING MY JOB, THE PROSPECT of building my own business was actually very exciting. My survival instincts kicked in. Remember, I've always thought like an immigrant. I had saved money all along, and fortunately, when the WNJU job ended, I received a good exit package that was the equivalent of a year's salary. Part of the package included letting me keep the company car. I recalled that on another occasion my WNJU boss said to me, "When I was your age, I lowered my overhead and started a business." So I took a hard look at my financial reality and tried to figure out how to reduce my expenses and generate some cash to put into my start-up.

I lived in New York City; what did I need a car for? So I sold it. I moved out of my expensive Upper West Side apartment into a rent-controlled, fourth-floor walk-up in the East

SELF
MADE

GO GET
YOUR OWN
CHIPS!

.

Village, right above a dive bar called McSorley's. My studio apartment was tiny, but the rent was only three hundred dollars a month. In the late 1980s, the gritty East Village was the center of New York's punk scene, full of artists and interesting people—and slightly dangerous—but really exciting and energizing for a single girl in her twenties. My parents, though, were horrified.

In my WNJU job, I had to travel to Latin America to find programming for the station, so I decided that my new business would be a production company that created original Latino programming. Broadcasters were always looking for content, and nobody in the United States was creating programming that was authentically Latino. I saw a hole in the market, a need that wasn't being met—in other words, a good business opportunity.

For the next four years, my production company didn't make a penny. Seriously—not a cent. I was running around, trying to get other TV stations and networks to buy my ideas for shows, but nobody bit. Still, I refused to quit. Why? Because another thing my old boss had told me had stuck in my head: "When I was your age, I started a business, and it took me ten years to make money." "Well," I thought, "I'm only on year four." I was also proud and stubborn, and I had convinced myself that this was what I was meant to do.

In the meantime, I took a job working as a stringer—a freelance producer—for a CBS affiliate in Philadelphia where another former boss now worked. I produced segments that they could plug into the news. Between the money I made from that and my savings, and thanks to my reduced overhead, I got by.

LISTEN TO YOUR INNER VOICE, BUT STAY OPEN ENOUGH TO HEAR GOOD ADVICE

· · · ·

MY PARENTS THOUGHT I WAS INSANE. MY MOM WOULD CALL ME and say, "*Mi'ja,* your looks are fading. You need to find a husband. Why don't you take a job? *Toda la gente,* they try to give you jobs, and you keep saying no." But I wouldn't listen. The East Village was exploding with creative energy, and all of my friends were trying to turn their talents into careers; they were musicians and writers and playwrights. My life was exciting, but inside I felt like a failure. I had to admit that my dream of starting my own business wasn't happening. I had fights with God, angry prayers, where I'd ask, "God, can't you throw me a bone? I'm such a good girl, why are you against me? Just throw me one little piece of business? Something—anything—and I'll take it as a sign!"

I got my sign. One of my dear friends, Concepción Lara, became an executive at HBO, and she hooked me up. I was finally in the right place at the right time. HBO was preparing to launch in Latin America and needed guidance from someone who knew the market. I knew the market!

A few months later, Bernard Stewart, the head of ESPN

International, heard about my work with HBO and offered to hire me to help launch ESPN Latino. He wanted me to produce all of the promos and the color commentary for the network in Spanish. I said, "There's only one problem: I don't like sports. I know nothing about sports."

"Nely, this is a big deal," Bernard said. "I'm going to pretend I didn't hear you. Why don't you go get yourself a sports tutor for a month and learn everything you can about sports terminology, like you would learn a language. Go do it and come back and get the deal." It was great advice. I memorized sports terminology and came back, and we made the deal. ESPN gave me an office in Connecticut. I started putting together a channel, and ESPN was paying me well for it. I still didn't have my own chips, not really, but I was happy because I was making money and I was making progress.

Then Concepción moved from HBO to Fox, and she told the people there about my work with HBO and ESPN. Not long after, I got called for a meeting with a guy named Rupert Murdoch, the new owner of Fox, who had only recently come to Hollywood from Australia. I flew to Los Angeles, and Murdoch explained his vision for launching Fox networks all over the world. "I want you to help us launch all of the Fox channels in Latin America, which will require you to work for Fox full-time."

Without even thinking, I replied, "I don't want to do that. What I really want is to produce the TV shows for these channels. I want to be a TV producer." Instead of making my own content, he wanted me to make promos and marketing materials for other people's content.

"You're wrong," he said. I was stunned. "Distribution comes before content. If you really want to be the queen of content, you need to be one of the key players of these channels."

I sat there feeling as dumb as a box of rocks. He was trying to tell me that you have to walk before you fly. Everybody wants to make TV shows, but I needed to prove myself by doing the meat-and-potatoes TV work first. That was the job he was offering me. It was not sexy, but it was lucrative.

I'd been stuck for four years. I couldn't get my business off the ground. What I didn't realize was there was something wrong with my business model. Then somebody who really knew the business spelled it out for me. And what's important is that I heard him. Murdoch became my mentor. I understood that he was right and that I needed to adjust my approach. In business, that's called "pivoting." It is very rare that a brand-new entrepreneur goes from zero to sixty without having to pivot. We now know that in the digital age it is almost impossible to succeed without revamping your approach numerous times before you get it right and everything clicks.

I accepted Murdoch's offer, but instead of coming inside Fox and working for him as an employee, I negotiated a deal where Fox would outsource the business to my company. It was a bigger version of my deal with ESPN. What chutzpah! How did I negotiate this deal? Little immigrant Nely could never have done it, but I chose myself, acted as if, and hot-wired confidence. I thought, "What would my WNJU boss do in this moment?" and I made the deal.

Fox became my biggest client, plus I still had the ESPN and HBO gigs. I officially launched Galán Entertainment in 1994 and overnight had to hire lots of employees. I had three major clients that I was servicing on two coasts. I moved from New York to Los Angeles. After years of nothing, it all took off. When you have big-name clients, everyone else starts to call. The next four years of my life I barely remember because I worked so hard. I traveled constantly and spent more time in Latin America than in the States. Although it sounds very glamorous, I promise you it was not. It was a lot of schlepping. I didn't change my lifestyle and start living large. I shared an apartment in L.A. with a girlfriend, and I invested every penny I made in real estate. More on that later.

I AM SELF-MADE: Joy Mangano

EVEN AS A YOUNG GIRL, JOY MANGANO, THE IN-spiration for the hit movie *Joy,* loved inventing solutions to problems. She studied accounting and, after graduation, found herself working as a waitress and an airline reservation manager to support her three children after a divorce. While trying to keep her house in order, she grew frustrated with how dirty and messy ordinary mops were. She saw a clear problem and invented a solution—the self-wringing Miracle Mop. Joy took her savings and investments from family and friends and used that capital to create a prototype and produce a run of a hundred units. She sold them at local trade shows on Long Island and eventually made a sale of a thousand mops on consignment to QVC. The sales started off soft, but Joy knew there were more sales to be had; no one knew how to sell her product better than she did. She persuaded QVC to let her on air to make her own sales pitch, and she was able to sell eighteen thousand mops in less than half an hour. She went on to become one of the most successful inventors and sellers on QVC and now has an empire built on Joy.

FOMO IS TOUGH,
BUT IT'S PART OF THE JOURNEY

• • • •

HERE'S THE TRUTH: WHEN YOU TAKE THE JOURNEY TO BECOM-
ing self-made, you will miss a lot of parties and fun times.
You will find yourself working late into the night when everyone else is out to dinner. You will be doing double duty—
doing your job and using vacation time to develop your side
business, while others are enjoying themselves on vacation.
Friends and family will give you a hard time for being such a
workaholic, and you will wonder, "Is this all there is? When
will all of this work pay off? When do I get to have fun?" You
will experience FOMO (fear of missing out).

Don't get discouraged. I promise you the party is where
you are, because you are working and building something.
Ask yourself, "Do I want to spend my life watching what
other people are doing? Or do I want to do what other people
watch?" Think about that.

It took me four years of knocking on doors and pulling
all-nighters to get to the point where I finally had my own
chips. But statistics show that most women give up their
dream of entrepreneurship in the second year. I want to improve the odds of female entrepreneurs making it to the finish
line; that's my motivation to teach what I've learned in my
journey. Succeeding as an entrepreneur is not easy, but I don't
regret one moment of it. Getting my own chips was the best
decision that I ever made, and I hope I can persuade you to do
it too.

QUESTIONS TO ASK YOURSELF BEFORE YOU GET YOUR OWN CHIPS

· · · ·

1. **Do you have enough money in the bank?**

When you are starting a business, you will go through periods in which little or no money is coming in. In order to be able to hang in there until you have a chance of success, you need to have a financial cushion that can carry you until you foresee bringing in enough money for your business to sustain itself. I recommend starting with at least one year, but preferably two years, of income saved. And yes, it can be done!

2. **Can you cut your expenses and reduce your overhead?**

Are you paying too much for your home or apartment? Can you live with a relative or share with a friend? Can you get by without a car? Do you really need that fancy gym membership? Can you cook at home instead of going out to expensive restaurants?

3. **Can you overcome your pride and fear of rejection?**

I had connections, and I wasn't afraid to use them. I swallowed my pride, but it wasn't always easy. Remember that you have nothing to lose by being confident and assertive and nothing to gain by being passive or shy. Even if the answer you get is no, you will be respected for going after what you want.

4. Do you have a financial backup?

I had a skill—reporting—that allowed me to work freelance and make money while I was building my business. My side gig was anonymous, and most important it didn't interfere with my main business. And what you do on the side can actually build your base of contacts and help you acquire skills you might not otherwise have.

5. Can you pivot and change course when needed?

After my conversation with Rupert Murdoch, I was willing to accept that someone else knew more than I did. If I did all of this again today, I would have hired a coach to help me with my business plan. Learning to refocus will serve you well. You may have to pivot several times over the course of your working life.

6. What's your competitive edge?

I had a skill—I spoke Spanish—and used it to my advantage. I had also run a TV station. These two assets made me unique at the time; not many people in the

TV world were bilingual. What is unique about you, and how can you exploit it to give you a competitive edge?

7. Do you have flexibility about where you live or work?

Are you willing to pick up and move wherever there is opportunity, where there may be an emerging business or market?

8. Are you willing to sacrifice for your dream?

I didn't buy new clothes for the four years I was starting my business. I had four basic outfits that were my uniform (I learned to love a uniform in Catholic school). I didn't spend money on expensive trips or cars or jewelry. Instead, I sacrificed. Bear in mind too that sometimes when you're working toward your dream, your personal life will take a backseat.

9. Are you in it for the long haul?

It took me four years to get to the place where I owned a thriving business. I worked day and night, and I never gave up. I did not let setbacks—and there were many—discourage or stop me. My belief in what I was doing was strong enough to keep me going. There will be obstacles to surmount, people in your way, unforeseen circumstances that can set you back. But you have to be prepared to weather the storms (see question No. 1), and your conviction about your goal has to be secure enough to power you through.

CHOOSING
A MENTOR

. . .

I'VE HAD MANY MENTORS IN MY LIFE, BUT I'VE NEVER asked a single one of them if they'd fill that role. Let's be honest: A successful, high-powered person is probably not going to feel as if he or she has the free time to mentor you—so don't bother asking! It took a while for me to realize that I didn't actually need permission; I could choose the person I wanted to be my mentor, observe him or her, and model myself after him or her.

I consider Warren Buffett a mentor, although I've never met him! He is one of the richest men in America, but he's also very grounded. His attitude toward wealth is understated; he doesn't own boats or private planes. I'm sure he has nice things and lives a very comfortable life, but he has committed his wealth to a higher purpose. I read everything he writes, I watch all of the interviews he does, and I consider him my self-appointed mentor.

Suze Orman is someone I considered a mentor long before I ever met her. Her teachings have been essential to my understanding the power of money in my life. I've read all of her books, watched her television shows, and attended her lectures. As a speaker and now a writer, I've been inspired to follow her lead and to add my own cultural twist to her teachings.

If someone you work with inspires you and you would like that person to be your mentor, volunteer to do her a favor. Stay late at the office, strike up a conversation, something that will afford you the opportunity to spend time with that person, to listen in on her conversations, and observe how she operates in different situations. Be like a sponge.

There is an endless menu of mentors you can choose from—family members, co-workers, people on social media. A mentor can be anyone who can offer a blueprint for becoming the person you want to be. Challenge yourself; ask, how can I incorporate what these people know into how I act and think? What would they say? What would they do? Soon the people you have admired and absorbed are all walking with you. The day you find your own voice, you've arrived at a very self-made place, because now you are ready to become a mentor for others!

SELF MADE

DO I WANT TO SPEND MY LIFE WATCHING WHAT OTHER PEOPLE ARE DOING?

OR

DO I WANT TO DO WHAT OTHER PEOPLE WATCH?

in your pain is your brand.

'M A BIG FAN OF THE CHICANA WRITER SANDRA CISNE-
ros. She's probably best known as the author of the classic
The House on Mango Street, but she's also an award-winning
poet, novelist, and creative writing teacher and the recipient
of a MacArthur Fellowship—also known as "the genius
grant." To me, she seems to write from the very depths of her
soul, and her language is raw and full of emotion and burns
with an incandescent truth. She and I became friends years
ago, and she encouraged me to take one of her writing workshops. She thought that I had the voice of a powerful Latina
and I should find a way to express myself through writing.

"How do I write about things that are too painful for me to talk about?" I once asked her.

"In your pain is your answer" was her reply.

I'll never forget that moment. What she meant was that if you want to create transcendent work—writing that strikes a universal chord with people—you have to go to the most unspeakable moments of your life. You have to write from a place that is so scary that your impulse is to run away. That is where you will find your truth. If you can create from that place of honesty, your work is bound to resonate with others.

Pema Chödrön, an American Buddhist nun whose work I greatly admire, has a powerful way of describing our relationship with pain. In her book *When Things Fall Apart,* she explains that whether you like it or not, pain is coming; it's inevitable. We can all be guaranteed pain in this lifetime. But she believes that place of pain is where we must go to find our true calling and our mission in life.

I believe that pain is a gateway to growth. As much as we may try to sweep pain under the rug, delete it, or shield our children from it, pain is something that we must learn to have a relationship with. When it arrives, it is terrible—that we know—but it's important to be aware that something great can come of it.

In terms of my own career, I came to see that my biggest successes have come out of the toughest, most painful experiences in my life. I grew up knowing the pain of being an immigrant and what it is like for a family to learn to navigate life in a new culture. I turned that pain into my particular expertise. I made a career in the Latino television market, helping launch ten U.S. channels in Latin America, translating content and promotional concepts for this market. That led to the opportunity to run Telemundo. Later I went on to produce hundreds of shows, many about Latinos and the stories of immigrants and their children in America.

Later in my career, I produced a reality show for Fox called *The Swan,* and again I channeled my pain. After I'd split up with my son's father, I was at a low point in my life; I was a single mom, I felt ugly and fat after having a baby, and I felt very much alone. But I got in touch with that pain, and I used it to connect with other women out there, making them feel less alone and less like ugly ducklings as they watched the journeys of the contestants who were given makeovers on the show.

Another touch point of pain for me has been my struggle to forge a path as a female entrepreneur. I've had to learn to do things my own way, I've had to fight at times to be taken seriously in an industry dominated by men, and I've had to learn to accept and deal with obstacles and setbacks and the realities of fear and failure as inevitable parts of my journey. It has never been easy, but what has grown from my pain is my mission: to empower women through entrepreneurship. Imagine if I hadn't had the courage to confront this pain! This is why I say that you can't run from your pain. You have to face it head-on.

We all struggle with our fears; we wrestle with our demons. It's human nature to try to avoid pain or deny that it even exists. But no one can really avoid pain. It connects us all. It's a shared dimension of the human condition. Women tend to respond to painful experiences differently than men, and I think this gives us a great advantage because we're not as afraid to talk about our experiences. We're not as afraid to move toward places of pain, and we're not as afraid to share our stories with others. I find that men, because of the way they're raised and the way we're all socialized, have a much harder time confronting pain. In my experience, when a man comes face-to-face with a painful, life-changing event, like a health scare or the loss of a loved one or a struggle with addiction, the tendency is to try to be stoic, to bottle it up, to push it down. There is cultural resistance to a man being vulnerable.

This is a huge advantage for women in the entrepreneurial space. I tell women at my events, "In your pain is your brand." I can take a woman's story of pain and turn it into a business idea. The first thing many of them tell me is the pain story that prevents them from reaching their goals. "My husband left me, and now I have to support my whole family." "I was physically abused." "I was emotionally abused." "I got laid off." "My husband got laid off." "I have a kid with disabilities." "I hate my job, but I have to take care of my parents." "I was in an accident and couldn't work for a year, and now I have horrible debt." They allow their pain to hold them back. (It's much different from what I have observed among men, who would rather just pretend that the painful event never happened.) I say to these women, "Honey, we all have a pain story." Because we do!

"Yeah," they will say, "but you haven't heard *my* pain story."

"Well, I promise you," I tell them, "there isn't a painful story you can tell me that I can't turn into a business."

I know this might sound bizarre and counterintuitive, but it's absolutely true: Pain is the gateway to your brand and your success. No matter what you've been through, you can build a business from your pain, because you are the expert in it and you are not alone in your experience of it. When you turn your pain into a business, you use your experience to solve a problem from which other people can benefit.

I tell these women to start, then solve a problem from their pain, and then find an audience for that problem. Here are a few real-life examples:

- There's the woman whose parents were deaf, and she spent lots of time helping them and translating for them and felt as if she had no time to find her own calling. I told her she had the calling: Start a translation service for deaf people. And she did!
- I met a woman at one of my Adelante events who was missing a leg and didn't have money for a proper prosthetic. I encouraged her to start a Kickstarter campaign to get the funds to get a proper limb, which she did. And then she realized that was the business she should begin: She could help people in Latin America source proper-fitting prosthetic limbs.
- I also met a Dreamer—a child of undocumented immigrants born in the United States—who started a blog to help other Dreamers learn their rights and how to navigate the system to get protected Deferred

Action for Childhood Arrivals, or DACA, status and work permits. The blog has sponsorship from organizations that support Dreamers and throws off revenue for the blogger.

the pain of discrimination

When I was seven years old, I came home from school crying because some kid had called me a "spic." I didn't know exactly what it was, but I knew it was bad and meant to hurt me. I told my mother.

"Oh, I am so sorry that little boy is ignorant," she said. I didn't know what "ignorant" meant either, but I knew it wasn't good. "You come from a beautiful country, and you speak two languages. You have the best of both worlds because you are an American and you are a Latina."

In these polarized times, it seems that someone at every event asks me whether I've ever been discriminated against in my career. Of course I have been, but I've never allowed it to get in the way of my success. For me, my dual identity is everything: It's the *reason* I am successful, it's the lens through which I see the world, it's my expertise, and I've built a career on it. If you're a woman of color or an ethnic woman, you understand what I'm talking about. It's not that it isn't painful to be discriminated against—it's what you do with that pain. And I choose to use it as firepower.

And then I remind myself, as my *mami* said, the people who don't get it are ignorant!

SEEING YOUR PAIN THROUGH THE EYES OF AN ENTREPRENEUR

• • • •

SPOTTING AN OPPORTUNITY TO TURN YOUR PAIN INTO YOUR brand isn't as hard as it sounds if you look at the world through the eyes of an entrepreneur. What are the elements of a great business? Here are some critical things to consider:

- **LOOK FOR A HOLE IN THE MARKET.** There might be an opportunity you can spot because of your sensitivity to a particular subject that would not occur to someone who hasn't had a similar experience. What is the experience that defines you, that makes you unique? What is everyone else missing? When I began making Latino TV shows, I had just come from HBO, where I had been taught to tell a story that only you can tell. I asked myself, "What story can I tell at Telemundo that someone at ABC could never tell?" I knew that I could tell the story of a Cuban woman who marries a Mexican and the cultural conflicts that arise between the in-laws. A major network wouldn't even know the differences between a Cuban and a Mexican family. But because I'd lived through it myself, I could tell that story.

- **IDENTIFY THE PEOPLE OUT THERE WHO SHARE YOUR PAIN AND NEED YOUR BUSINESS.** You are not the only person in the world who has gone through this painful experience. Others who have shared your struggles need information and support. How can you help these people and fulfill their needs with your business? Is your business a service that matches bilingual doctors with patients who don't speak English? Is it a business that offers affordable child care to single working mothers?

- **CREATE A BRAND THAT YOU CAN REPRESENT BETTER THAN ANYBODY.** At Telemundo, I was telling stories about immigrants and their kids. I knew that pain firsthand, so the shows were authentic. And the same thing goes for my Self-Made brand today: I am a self-made woman. This is the big advantage in marketing a product or an idea that is personal to you. When you build a business from your pain, you are naturally very passionate about it. You're going to think creatively, solve problems, and hang in there when things get tough because your idea and your business are your heart and soul. That adds a huge amount of value to any brand. It's an absolute element for success.

I AM SELF-MADE: Adele Horowitz

ADELE HOROWITZ CUT HER TEETH MANAGING other people's businesses, including her father's camera company in Manhattan. When she was young, her father would often say, "You're going to make a great secretary someday," and she would insist, "No, Daddy, I want to run your business." It would take a few more years and a problem that needed solving to fully ignite her entrepreneurial spirit.

As a young mother, Adele was shocked when her daughter was sent home from school with lice. The prevailing wisdom was that it was necessary to use shampoos laden with harsh chemicals to get rid of the bugs. Adele was horrified by the idea of lathering up her kid with a toxic solution, so she turned to the Internet for advice. After much research and a summer of trials, Adele came up with a foolproof way to get rid of lice that was completely natural and effective.

Through her pain, she identified a need—a safe treatment to rid children of lice—and created her brand, Licenders. She opened a salon in Manhattan that uses heat tools and her own formula of all-natural, enzyme-based shampoos, which she also sells online. In 2001 she applied for a $4,000 microloan from Count Me In, which she quickly repaid. She got contracts with schools, checking kids when they returned from vacations. She's gotten lots of press and her word-of-mouth referrals grew and grew. In 2011 she opened six more Licenender salons in the New York area. Her e-commerce business is robust. In 2012 she reported revenue of more than $1.5 million. Lately Adele has new hurdles to overcome because competitors are entering her space. The lice business has become hot! She responded by turning Licenders into a franchise and is currently in negotiations with several franchisees. A great "in your pain is your brand" success story!

TRANSCENDING PAIN

· · · ·

BEFORE YOU CAN MOVE PAST THE PAIN AND SEE IT AS SOME-thing other than an obstacle, you have to accept it. This is what I'd like you to understand: If painful things hadn't happened to you, you wouldn't be who you are now. You don't experience pain and come away unchanged.

Next, it's necessary to be willing to revisit the pain in your past to begin the healing. You have to examine the difficult relationships, jobs, and events of your past. As I said earlier, I believe that life is a puzzle that reveals itself slowly. If you look closely, often you'll see a pattern, or you'll recognize a cause-and-effect relationship: If A, B, and C hadn't happened, you might not have been prepared for E and F. Through introspection, you attempt to put the pieces of the puzzle together.

The easiest way to do this is to talk about it with someone you trust. For me, it came from working with a therapist, and I came away wishing I'd started therapy much earlier in my life. But for you, it might be working with a life coach or even just confiding in a trusted friend. If you want to explore therapy but you're worried about the expense, I want to tell you that it can be affordable and more accessible than you think. It may be covered in part by your health insurance, but another option is to investigate graduate programs in psychology in your area. There are plenty of psychology grad students in most cities who offer therapy sessions for free as a part of their course work. I'd recommend you seek out a practitioner of cognitive behavioral therapy (CBT). CBT is action oriented—it's like life coaching—and is in line with what I'm asking you to do in this book: You take action first, and your thinking and behavior will follow suit.

MAKING AMENDS WITH YOUR PAST

. . . .

WHEN I WAS IN GRADUATE SCHOOL FOR PSYCHOLOGY, ONE OF my professors gave us an interesting assignment. He asked us to make a list of all the resentments we've harbored against different people throughout our lives. People who abandoned you, or screwed you in a deal, or stopped being your friends and wouldn't return your phone calls. Then he asked us to make a list of the people we might have hurt. I've appropriated this exercise and worked it into my seminars. I ask my entrepreneurs in training, who are the terrorists of your life? The people who, when they show up in your life, it's as if they've got emotional grenades under their jackets, and you think, "I can't even be in the same room with this person!" Then ask yourself, who are the people who may feel that way about you? Maybe it's not your fault. Maybe you were a manager, and you had to fire someone. In my case, I think about men I've broken up with. When you make that list of who your terrorists are and whom you have terrorized, what you may find is that the list of those you have terrorized is the longer one.

Making amends is an important step in becoming self-made. Sometimes it helps you to apologize to those you have hurt. You can write a letter telling the person everything you feel. You don't have to actually send the letter; maybe the very act of acknowledging that you hurt someone, or that he or she hurt you, is enough to come to terms with what happened and move on. In the process, you might think of these stories of hurt differently and wonder, "Were they really hurting me intentionally?" We're all human, we're all doing the best we can, and we can't afford to allow past hurts to hold us back in our growth. This exercise is a way of clearing the slate. It's about purification. It is about readying yourself for a commitment to change, to evolve.

Whether you mail that letter or burn it and perform a ceremony that sends those wrongs away in a cloud of smoke, the bottom line is to take yourself out of the victim position. The work you're doing is about getting to a point of self-reliance and being responsible for where your life takes you. You are not the victim of your life experiences.

EXERCISE:

Turn Your Pain into Something Great

Think of three painful experiences from your life, big or small, that have affected you. Write about each of these experiences, capturing as much detail as possible. You can jot these things down as notes; you don't have to craft a perfect story, but try to include what you went through physically and emotionally. Make a note of anything you wish you'd done differently. What was the outcome you'd hoped for? Who else was involved, and how did they respond—or fail to respond—to your situation? What went wrong? What did people miss?

Now, imagine a similar scenario in which things go better. In this version of the story, what did you or someone else do to alleviate the pain you experienced? What was the solution? Is it a new kind of company or product? Is it an app? Could the solution be a community or support group that's built around this pain?

Finally, can you see a way to turn this pain into profit? Is there a business you can come up with that will serve this pain and the audience for this pain in a way that helps?

I AM SELF-MADE: Gloria Arredondo

GLORIA ARREDONDO'S PARENTS DIVORCED WHEN she was five years old. She has a memory of clinging to her father's legs, begging him not to leave, even though he was an alcoholic and had not been very present since she was born.

Gloria immigrated to the United States from Guanajuato, Mexico, at the age of fourteen with her mother and two siblings. She arrived not speaking English, but she was so bright and hardworking that in just two years she graduated from high school and began taking classes at the local community college. She received an associate's degree at the age of eighteen and earned a scholarship to the California State University, where she studied mechanical engineering. She was the only woman in the program and the only Hispanic. She graduated in 2001.

Sadly, she married a man who was physically abusive and stayed married to him for fourteen years, only separating from him when *he* asked *her* for a divorce. Gloria desperately wanted to keep the family together because of their child, who has special needs.

After her husband left, it took Gloria over a year to make sense of things. She realized that during her marriage she had stopped loving herself. She'd see her reflection in the mirror and feel as if she were looking at a monster. She couldn't stop gaining weight. She hated the person she'd become.

Gloria realized that her whole life she'd molded herself to fit the needs and wants of someone else. To address the changes she wanted to make in her physical body, she had the good instinct to engage the services of bodyworkers trained to treat victims of trauma. Letting go of the physical abuse and pain that were trapped in her body helped when nothing else had. It also sparked the idea for a business.

She attended workshops and seminars where she learned various techniques for emotional healing. She was hooked. She realized everything that had happened in her life brought her to this moment and she could use the pain to help others. She got trained as a trauma bodyworker and is now in private practice. She has written several books, gives lectures, and hosts a radio show on the subject in which she has unique expertise.

life is about your mission and your money.

YOUR MISSION IS WHATEVER GIVES YOUR LIFE PURPOSE and meaning and brings you joy.

Your money is what you do to support yourself and your family.

Your money and your mission are roads that you travel in your life, and they don't always align. They might run on two parallel tracks for years, until the day that you have enough money to dedicate your energy and your resources exclusively to your mission. If you're lucky, your mission also makes you money. But that's rare. And you can't afford to sacrifice your money for your mission—until, that is, you have enough money. Got it?

To be clear: *Money must come first, in order to fulfill your mission.*

Listen to me: You don't have to love every single thing you do at every stage in your life. There are plenty of things that we do to advance our careers that we don't necessarily love. Maybe you are naturally good at something that makes you money, but it's not necessarily your passion. But you know what? It can be fulfilling to make money at something you're naturally good at while you cultivate what you love on the side.

Learning how to balance mission and money is especially important when you're young and at the start of your career. At this stage, while you're doing whatever it is you need to do to make money, you should also be cultivating your mission whenever you can. Cultivate it. Cultivate it. Cultivate it. They say it takes ten thousand hours to develop mastery. That's a rough estimate. If your mission is to be a writer or an actor, chances are you are not going to make money at it right away, so you need to have a way of making money while you develop the skills you need to pursue your passion.

In my career in the entertainment business, I've seen too many creative people focus solely on their mission, only to starve for a couple of years and then give up. They might not have been so quick to give up their dreams if they'd had financial plans to support their evolution as artists. The more support you have, the more likely it is that you'll be able to cultivate your bliss in the long term.

Here's a great true story of mission and money: Jeremy Renner, star of *The Hurt Locker* and *The Bourne Legacy,* has twice been nominated for an Academy Award, but when he was an aspiring actor, he didn't want to be stuck in a place where he was starving and forced to take roles he didn't want. So to build a financial cushion that would allow him to wait for the right role, he started working in construction. He worked for a group of Latino contractors, and he learned the trade really well. As a bonus, he learned Spanish. And he worked among people who had backgrounds and life experiences that were different from his, that he could observe closely and use in his acting work. After a while, he took the money he made from his construction work and saved up enough to start buying cheap houses in underserved neighborhoods in L.A. During the week, he would work on the Latino construction crew, and on weekends he would work on renovating his own houses. He eventually started flipping houses and making money. Plus, his construction work allowed him a flexible schedule so he could put his construction jobs on hold when he had acting work. Eventually, he was making enough money acting that his mission and his money aligned.

I love Jeremy's story because it's a perfect illustration that sometimes your mission and your money can evolve as you evolve, from totally separate to occasionally crossing paths to completely aligned. Everyone is different and has to find his or her own formula for juggling mission and money, but it's definitely possible. Just ask Jeremy Renner.

I AM SELF-MADE: Mariah Kirstie

HERE'S ANOTHER TWIST ON THE JEREMY RENNER story. Mariah Kirstie is a twenty-four-year-old aspiring actress from Los Angeles. In the summer of 2015, she was out of work, trying to land a job that would bring in a stable income, but she needed some immediate cash flow to keep her afloat. Like Jeremy, she wanted to find a way to generate money that would allow her to take classes and break away for auditions.

Mariah took stock of every skill and asset that she had in her "toolbox." She had a car and a license, she liked to drive and knew the city well, so she realized that she had the means to turn all the driving she did into income. She signed up as an Uber driver and began to earn money from week one.

In time, Mariah also took a job as a sales associate for a Nike store, but she has continued driving for Uber to supplement her income. She now has two jobs running on her money track, with her mission—acting—running parallel. In the meantime, her acting career has taken off. She has a supporting actress role in the forthcoming movie *The Track*, which will compete in film festivals in 2016.

"FOLLOW YOUR BLISS" IS BS

. . . .

THESE DAYS, I CONSULT WITH COMPANIES AND ORGANIZATIONS on diversity and women's issues. My work has taken me all over the world; in the past year alone, I've traveled to Cambodia, India, Africa, and the Middle East. Everywhere I went, I saw women and their families running businesses together, and that really inspired me. I saw people working hard to raise themselves up to a place where they could realize their dreams. In their eyes, I saw hope and determination. I was in awe of their energy and resourcefulness. They were doing everything and anything they could to improve their situations and make their lives better.

As I observed these hardworking people, I thought about a phrase we hear a lot in America: "Follow your bliss." We're told, "Follow your bliss, and the money will come. Follow your bliss, and the universe will take care of you." The adage is attributed to the scholar Joseph Campbell, who wrote *The Power of Myth,* but Campbell's actual quotation is "Follow your bliss and don't be afraid, and doors will open where you didn't know they were going to be."

There's an important distinction here.

The popular American notion—that if you do what you love, success will surely follow—is, to put it bluntly, an entitled, First World way of thinking about success. It's a close relative to "wishing makes it so." Were the families I saw on my trip who were striving for a better life following their bliss? No! What I saw was a willingness and determination to work hard, a can-do, must-do attitude that I could really relate to. These people weren't waiting for anyone or anything to take care of them; they were taking charge of their own lives.

It occurred to me that women in emerging countries are better prepared for the Self-Made revolution because they are already on the front lines of the battle for self-sufficiency. They didn't have a choice. Their reality demanded it, just like the women who come here from other countries to make a better life for their families. These women are too busy taking care of business to follow their bliss. That's the immigrant advantage: that combination of optimism and grounded values tied to the practical imperative to earn a living and improve yourself. These are the core ingredients of the American Dream.

I AM SELF-MADE: Kathy Murillo

WHEN KATHY MURILLO GOT MARRIED IN 1990, SHE and her husband dreamed of devoting their lives to art, writing, and music. To that end, they started producing housewares with Latino accents. By chance, they met a sales rep who took samples of their line to the trade shows in L.A. and New York. Soon, orders started pouring in from over three hundred accounts, and Kathy and her husband couldn't manufacture enough goods to meet the demand. With two young children and a sketchy business plan, they were forced to scale back their business.

Kathy quit the home goods business and took a job as a part-time file clerk in the features section at *The Arizona Republic*. She worked hard, and being in the newsroom inspired her to become a reporter, so when a news clerk position opened up, she applied, even though she feared she wasn't qualified for the job. Because her work ethic and enthusiasm had been noticed, she scored an interview, even though she didn't have a bachelor's degree—a clear prerequisite for the job. Kathy shone in the interview and was given the position.

Kathy loved being a news clerk, and that led her to dream of becoming a reporter. One day, when the editor was having trouble finding a reporter for a particular assignment, Kathy leaped at the chance, and before long she was being assigned stories. Around this time, the managing editor approached Kathy and told her that she needed to invest in herself: She should go back to school to get her degree. Kathy was hesitant because her family and job already took up so much of her time, but the editor insisted that it would be good for her, in the long term, and the paper offered to pay her tuition. Kathy went to night school for three long years and got a degree in journalism. She was promoted to features reporter and was given her own columns—on crafting and movies, two of her passions.

Kathy's crafts column was a hit, and in 2001 she started promoting herself—writing letters to local TV stations and blogging as Crafty Chica. She blogged about her life and the projects that she was working on, and she always made sure that she linked back to her crafts articles in *The Arizona Republic*. Soon the views on her articles began to grow, and people started taking notice. She appeared on the local TV news, and her craft column was syndicated. She regularly scanned the growing list of her followers on her Twitter account, looking for anyone in the media. When she'd spot someone with media ties, she would reach out to the person directly, looking for opportunities to promote the Crafty Chica brand. This scrutiny paid off big-time with a profile in *The New York Times*!

"I always waited until everyone was asleep, and then I worked on my business every night," Kathy says. That is the beauty of working online: You don't have to leave your house to make the magic happen! Her goal? She wanted to make craftychica.com the CNN of creativity! She used Tyra, Oprah, Martha, and J. Lo as her brand role models because they knew how to keep their products fresh and diverse. She began selling homemade Mexican-inspired crafts on her site, created Crafty Chica YouTube videos, and was offered a book deal. Soon she was invited to speak at a big national craft convention and got an offer to work on a product line for Michaels. Crafty Chica was in business!

Kathy left her newspaper job in 2007 to pursue Crafty Chica full-time. She was smart and strategic about her brand extension: She wrote seven craft books and two novels—published by major publishing houses—and she launched a web series for Lifetime online. Her Crafty Chica product line continues to be sold in Michaels, she leads an annual art cruise to Mexico, and she is developing a Crafty Chica giftware line of mugs, candles, and picture frames! She believes that identifying a market that is underserved—Latinas—and then filling that gap has been the secret to her success.

All of these enterprises were just daydreams that Kathy turned into goals and then action plans. She was single-minded and relentless. Take a lesson from Kathy: Embrace technology and all the resources the web has to offer; it's free! Pursue your passion (but keep your day job). This is your one and only life; take hold of it and celebrate your gifts and talents. Live a life you love. Go find your happy!

WHAT'S YOUR MONEY?
WHAT'S YOUR MISSION?

· · · ·

IF YOU WORK ON ALIGNING YOUR MONEY AND YOUR MISSION, IT won't be long before you start to see yourself differently. Because you will be different. Money and mission will be in balance in your life, and you will feel whole. So ask yourself the following questions:

MONEY

- What are your skills and natural abilities?
- How can these skills and natural abilities make you money?
- Is there a business you can start on the side that will make you money?

MISSION

- What do you love to do that you would do for free?
- Can you cultivate this thing, your mission, while also making money?

don't buy shoes,
buy buildings.

SEX AND THE CITY IS ONE OF MY ALL-TIME FAVORITE
TV shows. If you were a fan, I'm sure you remember Carrie
Bradshaw referring to her "substance abuse problem"—her
fabulous shoe collection. When she breaks up with her boyfriend, she realizes that she can't afford to buy her own apartment because she has spent every cent she's ever made on
Louboutins and Jimmy Choos. She goes to the bank and asks,
"Why can't you give me a loan? Look, I've made money." And
the banker says, "Shoes are not collateral for an apartment."

"Don't buy shoes, buy buildings!" I want to tell the Carrie
Bradshaws of the world. This is advice that I want women to

take literally: I really do want you to get out there and invest in buildings instead of spending money on disposable things like shoes, no matter how amazing they may be. But this advice is also metaphorical. When I tell you to buy buildings, I mean that I want you to have a big dream, an ambitious idea, something that you are really going for in life, instead of filling that hole with short-term gratification—a dress, a pair of shoes, more stuff you don't need.

If you are a millennial, I want your real role models to be people like my twentysomething friend Tara Winter in Los Angeles, who began thinking entrepreneurially in high school. Tara went to a Santa Monica school that was filled with the kids of celebrities, but she lived with her single mom, and they didn't have a lot of money. This girl was brilliant. She's an example of someone who, from an early age, was able to channel the pain of necessity and turn it into cash. She realized that everyone in her school was six degrees of separation from somebody in Hollywood, and many of her friends had mothers or aunts with closets full of costumes and designer clothes that they no longer needed. With her mother's help, Tara started an eBay store called fullcircle fashion.com that was like an online Hollywood resale shop. She'd tell the juicy, tantalizing backstory of these vintage clothes with their fancy pedigrees as gossipy blind items. "This dress has been on the red carpet with a long-legged A-list movie star," or "These killer shoes were worn by a blond soap opera actress who married her co-star." She would give the people who gave her the clothes 60 percent of the profits, and she'd keep 40 percent. Celebrities started contacting Tara directly through Instagram and Facebook because they loved how respectful she was of their privacy while still giving the clothes a fabulous showcase.

Tara got so good at doing business with almost no overhead that she's made enough money to pay her way through college. Now she is in her mid-twenties, married to her high-school sweetheart, and the mother of a one-year-old baby girl, and her business is still going strong. She was able to cover the down payment on their first home with her revenue from fullcirclefashion.com. Tara is the literal and figurative embodiment of the message in this chapter, because she used old Manolos and Jimmy Choos to buy a house!

FORGET BLING

· · · ·

ONE OF MY MENTORS IN THE ENTERTAINMENT INDUSTRY ONCE said to me, "I don't know what's up with you young people. As soon as you start making money, you use it to buy bling. You are all just living with bling." I think what he was trying to say was that he saw a lot of Latinos and African Americans buying jewelry and gold chains and expensive cars as soon as they became successful. I understand where he was coming from, but I fully understand the pain of coming from another culture and feeling like an outsider. Many of us who come from ethnic backgrounds that typically get profiled feel as if we have to "show" our money in order to be allowed into exclusive stores or clubs or even schools.

This same boss—who happened to be African American—also advised me to buy real estate. "If I had to do it all over again, that's what I would do," he said. "I would start buying buildings as soon as I could. And I would have bought my house last." When he told me this, it didn't make sense to me, because the conventional wisdom held that the goal was to own your own home. He explained, "I buy commercial real estate. You want to own property that brings you income. If you buy a building, you can rent it, and the rent provides you with income. You can buy yourself a house, but until you sell it, it is a drain on your resources. And you're emotional about it. Whereas if you rent a building, the tenants pay all the expenses of the building." I heard that once, and that was all it took. Lesson learned.

LOWER YOUR OVERHEAD,
PART II

· · · ·

INITIALLY, I DEVIATED SOMEWHAT FROM MY MENTOR'S ADVICE because I used the first money I made to buy a condo in Miami for my parents. Latinos believe in the importance of taking care of our parents first. It's our duty. I know this is also true for people from traditional families and cultures. For me, making sure that my parents were taken care of in their retirement was a badge of honor. After I bought that condo for my parents, I bought a building. Here's how.

When I went to work for Fox, I was offered the chance to

rent office space on the 20th Century Fox lot in Century City. I jumped at the opportunity because working on the lot was very glamorous and there were business advantages to it too. You'd go out to lunch, and you'd run into all kinds of movie stars and moguls. On the way to my car, I'd see Denzel Washington. I'd be running to a meeting and see the entire cast of *In Living Color,* including the young J. Lo. Or I'd walk by a soundstage and see them setting up a shot for *Speed* with Sandra Bullock and Keanu Reeves. For a while, I was in awe; I felt like I was a part of Hollywood history.

But the bills started coming in. They were charging me a fortune for this tiny office space! As these staggering rent bills kept arriving month after month, I thought, "Seriously? This is money that I could be saving or putting back into my business or investing!"

So I started looking to buy a building that could house my office. I was looking for an inexpensive place that was semi-close to the Fox lot. Everything pointed toward Venice, a funky beach town with actual canals . . . and a little gang-related violence. I thought it was supercool. Hey, I'd just moved out of the East Village . . . no big deal! In 1998, buildings in Venice were very cheap. One building in particular caught my eye. To call it a fixer-upper was an understatement; it needed to be gutted. But to me, it had potential. I discovered that a musician owned the building. He had bought it for pennies, and his plan was to turn it into a live/work space, with a music studio downstairs. When I inquired, he told me it was not for sale. Some time passed, and I kept looking, and then I read in a Hollywood trade publication that the musician had gotten a movie deal and was moving to London. Well, he didn't need the building anymore! So I got in touch with him again. I was persistent. Eventually, he wrote back and offered to sell it to me for one million dollars. I replied, "Are you kidding me? I'm a Latina. I know you bought that building for nothing. Are you trying to take advantage of me?" I guilt-tripped him, and eventually he sold it to me for practically nothing . . . plus 10 percent.

I was really excited that I'd managed to buy that building. But when I went back and told my staff, they freaked out. One woman said, "Nely, it's taken you so long to get to the place where you're on the Fox lot. Why would you want to leave all that prestige behind to go to some dump in Venice?"

"You say that because you think that the prestige of our company comes from 20th Century Fox," I told her. "But I'm the pioneer here. We have to think about what's best for our company, and what's best isn't having all of our cash flow go right out the door. We can visit the Fox lot all we want. If Fox ever stops doing business with us, what's our value? We have to build our own company and our own brand." She was speechless. She really didn't get it. In her mind, Fox was Prince Charming, and I was leaving the shiny studio castle to venture into an untamed forest.

If you had told me then that my building in Venice would allow me to retire in my forties, I wouldn't have believed you. But that's exactly what happened. In real estate, they say the normal trajectory for a property to fully appreciate in value, to the point where you can create positive income from it, is twenty to twenty-five years. But that building appreciated in

han ten years. The revenue from it and other buildings I
subsequently bought allowed me to dedicate myself full-
time to my mission. None of this would have happened if I
had continued to rent on the Fox lot, or if I had bought shoes
instead of buildings.

HAVE A VISION FOR YOUR LIFE . . . AND BE PREPARED TO SACRIFICE TO ACHIEVE IT

• • • •

IT'S IMPORTANT TO POINT OUT THAT IN MY EARLY YEARS, WHEN
I was first investing in real estate, I sacrificed a lot. I finally
did buy myself a house, but mostly I rented. And I didn't buy
fancy furniture. I did not go on lavish vacations. But remember, "sacrifice" is not the same as "suffer."

I was able to sacrifice in the short term because I had a
vision for my life. When I was in my late twenties and still
living in New York, I went out for my birthday with a bunch
of friends to one of those shops where you paint ceramics.
We each painted a ceramic tile with a scene of what we
wanted our future lives to look like. We had a great time, and
then I took my tile home and put it away. Over the years, I
completely forgot about the tile.

Two years ago, I was going through old stuff in my closet,
and I found the tile. I couldn't believe my eyes. There was a
house on the tile that was orange and an office that was hot
pink. And there was a dog. There was also a palm tree. On

the other side of the tile, I had written a wish list: I wanted a house that was paid off and a business that made me enough money to retire, and I wanted to go back to school. Today, my house and my office are famously colorful; they're tourist stops in Venice. I have a dog that I love more than life itself. And I fulfilled my dream of going back to school. I was astonished that my dreams and my goals, which I'd dared to set in stone (okay, tile), all came true. I showed the tile to Brian, and we cried hysterically.

"You're a psychic witch!" he said, between sobs.

"No, it's just that I had a vision and I made it happen," I said.

That's what I mean when I tell women that they need to have a vision of who they want to be that drives them forward and clear goals that will be their signposts along the way. You really have to know what you want, and you have to be willing to sacrifice to get it. But once you do, it will mean the world to you because you know that you earned it. Nobody gave it to you. It wasn't handed to you. It can't be taken away from you. You did it on your own. That feeling of self-reliance is transformative.

"Don't buy shoes, buy buildings" is very deep for me. It's a fun catchphrase, but it's no joke. It is something I have personally experienced, and it's a credo that I live by. And it leads you to important questions to ask yourself: *What is the vision I have for my life, and what am I willing to sacrifice to make that vision a reality?*

I AM SELF-MADE: Angie Henry

ANGIE HENRY WAS BORN IN MEXICO AND MOVED across the border with her parents and five siblings when she was a little girl. They settled in a small mobile home in San Diego. Space was so tight that Angie had no bed to call her own; she slept on the living room sofa.

"Growing up was definitely a struggle," she recalls. "My mom worked in greenhouses. She would come home with mud up to her knees and rashes on her hands and her neck from the pesticides." Her mother instilled in her children the importance of an education. "She'd say, 'You need to go to school,'" Angie remembers. "'You need to be successful.'"

Angie was able to attend a good public school in a fairly affluent area, but she felt different from the other kids. "The teacher would say, 'Today when you go home and you sit at your desk and do your homework...' In my mind, I couldn't help thinking, 'How am I going to do my homework? I don't even have a desk.'"

Angie got pregnant at sixteen, yet she finished high school and worked at a furniture store until she could afford to buy her own bed and desk and make plans for the future. Her dream was to have her own home.

One day, when Angie was in the shipping and receiving department, she overheard that there was a manufacturing order that involved sewing a pattern the company couldn't fill. Angie figured out how to sew the pattern; she was already an excellent sewer. She took and filled the order herself. Angie continued taking orders and eventually hired freelance sewers to help fill larger orders, many of which called for embroidery. With the money she made from her sewing side business, she put herself through college and bought a small house that could function as both a home and an office for her company.

In 2005, she went back to school and studied to get her realtor's license, which she got a year later. She joined NAHREP—the National Association of Hispanic Real Estate Professionals—and the San Diego County Hispanic Chamber of Commerce to make connections and find real estate jobs. She kept her embroidery business going while she took on jobs as a realtor. In fact, the embroidery supported her through the economic downturn in 2008.

Angie came to an Adelante event in Los Angeles, and she heard me say that women need to think like owners, not like employees. That struck a nerve with her. She realized that while she owned her own business, she was thinking like an employee when it came to her real estate career. She formed a new goal: to have her own brokerage firm, with other agents working for her. She knew that's where the real money would be.

Angie worked hard. She was smart, and her co-workers respected her. By the time she had saved enough money to open her own real estate firm, she had earned a repu-tation as a skillful and fair broker, so other realtors wanted to work for her. She rented space in a shared of-fice and was joined by four employees from the firm she'd worked for. Because she had so much experience in real estate, she was able to hire smart and leverage her contact base into immediate business. Soon, her broker-age was thriving.

Angie's advice for other women who want to be en-trepreneurs: "Follow your intuition and follow what your heart tells you to do. Stay focused and seek out network-ing groups and mentors that can help you and inspire you and lead you in the right direction."

On a personal level, Angie's self-made journey has enabled her to fulfill her dream and pass the torch. "Owning a home is part of the American Dream," she says. "Being able to give a family the keys to their new home is like being able to give them the keys to happi-ness. Through my work, I've been able to provide a bed and a desk for every single client who comes to me."

you have to sacrifice. and then sacrifice some more.

To MAKE IT TO THE FINISH LINE OF LIFE, YOU HAVE TO make money, save money, and invest money so that you make money while you sleep. More on this later, but for now what you need to know is that just making money won't get you where you need to go.

When I first started investing in real estate, I sacrificed a lot. I finally bought myself a house in Venice, but I rented it out for income because I was spending so much of my time in Latin America. I was working hard and traveled a lot for work. So I rented an apartment for the time I spent in L.A., and I knew that down the road there would come a time when I could turn to my house, furnish it in a way that reflected me, and enjoy living in it.

I did not go on lavish vacations. I did not in any way live a grandiose life. I sacrificed consciously. I could do this because I had a vision for my life. I told myself, *I can do this if I'm willing to be humble, to sacrifice, to be grounded. I am willing to be realistic and dream at the same time.*

Is it possible to have it all? That question has tormented generations of women since the dawn of the women's movement. I believe it is possible. You just can't have it all at the same time. There is a time in your life to sacrifice. And there is a time to enjoy the fruits of your sacrifice. But cultivating your dream means exchanging short-term gratification for long-term goals and learning to do it with joy and purpose. You will reap the rewards of your sacrifice in spades when you realize your dream.

EXERCISE:

Are You Ready to Become Self-Made?

Use the questions below to take stock of your life, piece by piece. What comes easily to you? What has always been a challenge? Where do you want to make changes? Give yourself time to ruminate on the questions fully and allow your mind to go where it goes; in other words, consider the questions below carefully *and* jot down anything that pops into your head.

o   *Give up the fantasy:* Have you let go of your rescue fantasy?
o   *Listen to fear:* Has it shown up lately? How is it guiding you to what you have to do? Have you pushed yourself to confront your fear?
o   *Choose yourself:* Are you declaring your-self? Discovering who you are? Thinking like an owner? Acknowledging that you are ready to become self-made?
o   *Take power:* Is there an opportunity for you to take power that you have been reluctant to act on? Why? What's holding you back?
o   *Use your pain to find your brand:* Have you figured out how to turn your pain into money?
o   *Invest in yourself:* What are you learning? How are you growing? Who is on your sup-port team? Whom do you need to add?
o   *Commit to your money:* What do you do to make money? How much can you put away?

IF I KNEW THEN WHAT I KNOW NOW . . .

Are you starting a business on the side, getting a second job? What skills do you have that you can monetize?

- o *Identify your mission:* Are you cultivating what you love? Is it inspiring you to put money away so you can achieve it?
- o *Embrace sacrifice:* What are you willing to give up for your long-term goals?

3.

■

HOW TO
BECOME
SELF-MADE

the goals, the game plan, and getting it done.

HE FIRST STAGE OF THE SELF-MADE JOURNEY IS AN interior one. In the first two parts of the book, I shared the emotional and practical education I received on my own path, the hard-won lessons that shaped my view of who I wanted to be and what I wanted to accomplish in this life. I asked you to begin to turn the ship of your mind and set it on a new course. To think differently. To approach virtually every aspect of your life with a new mindset and clearly defined priorities. I hope I've convinced you that there is no option but to choose yourself, to declare your intentions, to forge the self-made path, so that you can live a life that is rich in every way.

So what does it mean to live a rich life? I defined it at the beginning of the book, but it's worth repeating here as you prepare to embark on the next phase of the self-made journey.

It means being able to sleep soundly at night, without worries.

It means getting out of survival mode, where you're one problem away from catastrophe.

It means rewarding yourself and your children with things like an education, trips, and owning a home.

Eventually, it means being able to work because you want to, not because you have to.

When you live a rich life you feel empowered, self-reliant, self-actualized, and free.

Now, in order to get your mission and your money straight, to assess the skills you possess—the motor that will power you—and to bring your calling into focus—the big-picture aspirations that will fuel that motor—you have to make an inventory of your life.

MAP THE TRAJECTORY
OF YOUR LIFE

. . . .

WE TEND TO FORGET THAT EVERYTHING WE DO LEADS US TO the next place. Like everyone else, I've worked less than ideal jobs in my life, but those jobs helped get me where I am today. One of the most interesting and revealing things I did for myself early in my career, at a time when I was feeling stuck, was to draw up a chart that traced all the jobs I'd had until that point. Together, they gave me a tangible map, showing me precisely where I'd been and what I'd learned about myself and my abilities. Putting together that puzzle of my likes, dislikes, and skills was critical in helping me figure out the way forward. When you see it all in black and white, a picture begins to emerge. It's just as important to know what to eliminate from your life as what to keep and expand upon. If you feel hopeless because you're stuck in a job that you dislike, then you may not be looking at the big picture, and you may be allowing yourself to get buried in the moment instead of looking up and trying to plot your next move. This exercise is designed to give you some perspective.

Here is my chart:

JOB	LIKES	DISLIKES	SKILLS ACQUIRED
The Limited	• Making sales	• Doing inventory	• Sales • Organization
Seventeen	• Glamorous setting • Storytelling • Researching	• No money	• Researching • Storytelling • Thinking on my feet
Teen TV reporter	• Traveling • Interviewing interesting people • Being on TV	• Making no money • Bus travel • Bad hotels • Finding myself in dangerous situations	• Adapting to diverse circumstances and people • Communication skills • Gaining confidence in front of the camera • Technical skills • Teamwork • Storytelling

JOB	LIKES	DISLIKES	SKILLS ACQUIRED
News producer, CBS	• Action-packed • Seeing my work on the air every day • Diverse subject matter • Challenging	• Depressing subject matter • Rushed pace • Factory mentality • Rough lifestyle	• Performing on short deadlines • Making shows on low budgets • Understanding the importance of keeping up with current events • Editing
TV station manager	• Being the top dog • Community work • Hispanic market • Dealing with advertisers • Accounting—*who knew?*	• More technical than creative • Long hours • Managing a lot of people	• Running a business • Math!!! • Giving consumers what they want • Realizing the importance of profit

My takeaways? I liked running a business that connected with customers, that made money, that was creative, collaborative, and exciting. I wanted to engage with content that

SELF
MADE

WHEN YOU
LIVE A RICH LIFE
YOU FEEL
EMPOWERED,
SELF-RELIANT,
SELF-ACTUALIZED,
AND FREE.

.

was meaningful to people, particularly to my own community. I loved a good story. I liked upbeat people and upbeat material. I knew how to sell, how to think on my feet, how to call the shots for a whole company, and—very important—how to balance the books! I'd learned to love math! The next move for me was starting my own TV production company, delivering product to the Latin market.

Here is your chart to fill out:

JOB	LIKES	DISLIKES	SKILLS ACQUIRED

What are the takeaways for you? What's the next thing you need to learn to round out your education? What do you love? What can you get passionate about? What do you wish you could delegate to someone else? What is it that you and only you can do—better than anyone else? What industry attracts you? Service? Hospitality? Retail? Manufacturing? Technology? Fashion? Food?

The idea is that a picture starts to emerge—the puzzle of YOU starts coming together. The pieces of that puzzle will help you see yourself and your assets clearly and will help determine what kind of an entrepreneur you will be.

Let's say you're in your twenties and you're working as a waitress. You may feel that you're stuck in a crappy job. But if you can rise above the day-to-day for a moment, what are you learning on the job? For one thing, you are learning the workings of a restaurant. You see what the owner of this restaurant is doing right or wrong. You understand what it takes to provide excellent customer service and to keep your employees happy. You engage with customers face-to-face. You learn the costs of staff, overhead, food deliveries. Managing orders and efficiencies. You may see areas where the current owner could make improvements. Maybe you're thinking, "If I were in charge, here's what I'd do differently . . ." Maybe it inspires you to own your own restaurant. Maybe it inspires you to go to school to get a degree in management, the culinary arts, or business administration. With the next step and the next level of expertise and earning power, your acquired skills and ambitions change once more. Perhaps you're in the position to realize your dream of owning your own business by the time you're forty-five. Fifteen years later, the years of success in business can allow you to dedicate yourself, in your sixties, to running a nonprofit that speaks to your passion and your mission.

Tease out the puzzle pieces of your life and put them together. There's not one right configuration. There may be several. This is trial and error, with a purpose. I want you to see every stage as preparation for the next. This is an ascent—an accumulation of experience and knowledge, guided by the imperative to become an owner in every aspect of your own life, no matter where you are and what your job is. So it's not about finding the next job; it's about acquiring inner strength and clarity and purpose. Figuring out where you want to go with all these likes, dislikes, skills, talents, and abilities? That's the work of the next section.

SETTING GOALS

· · · ·

WHEN I ADDRESS GROUPS OF WOMEN AT EVENTS, I OFTEN BEGIN by asking them a question, even though at this point I can kind of predict the answer. So in that way, it's sort of a trick question, but I ask it with love in my heart, not to make them feel small. The question is simple: What are your goals? And more often than not, the answers they give me are the wrong answers. "I want to buy a new car." "I want to get out of debt." "I want to buy myself something really nice to reward myself." That's small-time stuff. Short-term gratification.

Women tend to think small. I gotta tell you, when you ask this question of men, they come back with much bigger answers. Why is that? That's something for sociologists and psychologists and biologists to answer; it may well be an evolutionary thing as much as a cultural one. And yet the culture changed radically for women in the past fifty or sixty years! So why haven't our ambitions changed at the same pace? Why have our dreams stayed so small and humble? I'm an optimist; I think we can make these changes consciously and rapidly if we shine a light on the problem. That's part of my mission in this Self-Made movement. We're here to change minds, starting with yours.

So here, now, I want you to dream big. Below, I'm asking you what your goals are, and I want you to think way beyond the short term when you commit them to paper. This is your secret list. Don't be embarrassed: This list is private; it's for only you to see. It's your North Star—no one else's. So let's be clear: We don't want short-term goals here. We want the goals you hope to achieve in twenty to thirty years.

As an example, these were my goals when I was in my twenties:

- Have two years of salary saved: one for emergencies and one to invest.
- Own my home outright—no mortgage.
- Own a building—a property I could rent out to generate income.
- Go back to school and get my degree.
- Have money saved for retirement.

- Send my child to college.
- Own a beach house in my country of origin.
- Take a trip around the world.
- Retire by age sixty-five.

I achieved all of these goals by the time I was forty-five. I was fortunate: I took advantage of opportunity, and I found the discipline and guidance to stay the course. And now I am reaping the rewards.

To help the women I work with come up with their goals, I guide them with this thought: Project way ahead, to the later years of your life, and work backward. Think of yourself and your life at eighty-five. How do you want to be at eighty-five? Do you want to be financially independent? Do you want to lead by example for your family—to show them what a strong and self-sufficient woman you are? There's something very clarifying about reckoning with your mortality; it is a motivator like no other. Millennial artist Candy Chang has become a social media sensation with her global art-wall project, called *Before I Die*. On Chang's walls, women of all ages share lists of things they want to do before they die. Candy's project has particularly resonated with young women. Also, a recent *New York Times* article by Arthur C. Brooks called "To Be Happier, Start Thinking More About Your Death" cited several studies that showed that when people were asked to contemplate their death, it focused and inspired them. It made their priorities crystal clear. You have to think big, because if you don't think big, you won't get there.

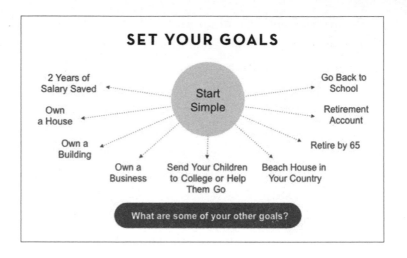

So I ask you, where do you want to be at eighty-five, sixty-five, fifty, forty, thirty? What are your goals?

What are your markers? How will you measure success? How will you know you've arrived at your goal?

Will you right the wrongs of your life as soon as you are able?

Do you want to lose weight and get healthy?

How much money do you want in the bank by the time you retire? How much money do you need to live per month—to live well without worries?

Take a look around at people you know who are not happy and resolved, who are struggling. Ask yourself, where in the trajectory of this person's life did things go wrong? What can you learn from these cautionary tales?

Where do you want to live? What do you want your house to look like?

Tough goals require stamina, but if it's not worth fighting for, it's probably not a worthy goal.

More recently, as I mentioned earlier, I set a goal for myself to lose weight and get healthy. How did I find the discipline and determination to not eat carbs for almost a whole year? I put up a picture in my house of me, twenty-five years younger, thin and smiling and wearing fancy clothes on the cover of a magazine. Next to it, I put a recent photograph of me, fat. If I didn't see the skinny picture and the fat picture every day—if I wasn't connected with the visual image of where I was and where I wanted to go—I'm not sure I could have stuck to the plan. I'm a big believer in visual aids to help manifest a goal. Vision boards, mood boards, look books, diaries, journals—whatever form it takes. You put the picture out there and it helps you realize your goals.

Make a vision board for yourself. It's a way of creating a concrete commitment, turning a concept into reality. It's another way of declaring yourself.

THE GAME PLAN

. . . .

NOW THAT YOU HAVE DEFINED YOUR GOALS, HOW ARE YOU GOING to achieve them? You're going to make money while you sleep.

When I first heard this phrase, it sounded like Chinese to me. I had no idea what it meant. But it is the most critical part of your self-made plan, and it gets to the entrepreneurial heart of becoming self-made. Ultimately, the objective is to

SELF MADE

MAKE MONEY WHILE YOU SLEEP.

.

come up with a business or a product or an investment that is a source of continuous income, that makes you money twenty-four hours a day, while you're off making more money in your job or, if you're fortunate enough, while you're off loving life and living out your dreams.

That internal motor that drives you toward self-reliance is also the engine of your entrepreneurial spirit. There are many ways that entrepreneurial spirit can play out in your life. How you choose to do it and become an owner in your life is up to you. But the absolute truth doesn't change: You need to make money, save money, and invest your money in something that makes money for you even when you're not working. Why?

Because you're not going to make it to the finish line on your salary alone.

Even professionals—like my friend the dentist—need a source of income that can provide for them after they stop working. Maybe for that dentist with her lucrative practice it is enough to invest the money she makes in a retirement account so that it can support her later in life. But maybe you don't have enough income to save and invest now. For most of us, we need to generate more money now to be able to have the money to invest, either in stocks or in real estate or in a business, investments that will provide for us for the rest of our lives.

First you make money. I want you to find a way to make more money—as in, more money than you are currently earning. Maybe it's starting a side business on eBay or Amazon. Maybe it's driving for Uber a few nights a week. Yes, I am asking

you to work even harder than you already do. I am asking you to sacrifice. Watch your spending. Lower your overhead.

Then you save money. Next, I want you to put away *every cent* you make in your second job. *The goal here is to save one year's salary.* You heard that right! One year of salary (at least!) is a cushion, an emergency fund. It is peace of mind. But don't save and quit; saving is a lifelong practice, and I promise you that you are going to learn to love it. Why save more than what you need to cover yourself in an emergency? To have money that you can put toward making more money.

Next you invest money. I invested in real estate and in a retirement account. It's very important to contribute to your retirement accounts! Invest that money so it grows. Compound interest is a

beautiful thing. For the first and last word in retirement planning, I urge you to read my friend
and role model Suze Orman's books: *Women &
Money* will change your life, and it will teach
you how to open, fund, and invest in a retirement
account. *The Money Class* will teach you everything you need to know about stocks, bonds,
IRAs, Roth IRAs. Take your pick; you will not go
wrong. I want you to be a beautiful, happy, secure old lady.

Once your retirement account is funded and you're out of
debt, you're ready to invest your money in a vehicle that will
make money while you sleep.

MATH DOESN'T LIE

· · · ·

MATH IS FUN. ADDING UP MONEY IS FUN! IF I LEARNED TO LOVE
math, you can too! Why do you have to love math? Because
math is going to take us home.

The good news is that doing the math is very straightfor-
ward. Money is not sentimental, it is not emotional, it won't
say nasty things behind your back. The numbers in your bank
account speak for themselves. Math doesn't lie. And when
you are in control of your money, there is no greater high.
Financial power is true freedom, and math is your best friend.
It will not betray you.

HOW TO SAVE ONE YEAR OF SALARY

1. Fall in love with saving money and watching it grow. Learn to love the feeling of depositing money in the bank. It's way more fun to watch your money grow than the alternative: to worry and grow anxious and lose sleep as your money dwindles away.

2. Get out of debt. You can't move forward if debt is holding you back. Come up with an aggressive plan for paying down your debt, including student loan debt (which cannot be discharged in bankruptcy). If you start a side business to generate extra cash for savings, put 50 percent of what you earn toward debt and 50 percent toward savings. Watching your debt come down as your savings grow will inspire you.

3. How to save? Sacrifice. Save a minimum of 20 percent and up to 50 percent of what you earn. Begin by writing down the amount of money you take home every month. What is 20 percent of that amount? Write it down. Commit to that number. I know what you're going to say: There's just no way! I live in an expensive city, my rent is high, I can't save! And here's what I am going to say back to you: Decide that you are going to stop spending everything you make. Pretend that you make less than you do. Reduce your expenses. What can you downsize? Be strict about new spending. No new spending! Post your goals somewhere in your house where you can see them every day. Remind yourself that this short-term sacrifice is going to buy you freedom and peace of mind later in life. Don't buy shoes . . .

4. Start a business on the side and save 100 percent of that money. If you want to save faster, this is what you have to do. You have a business calling out to you right in your own home.

START A BUSINESS IN YOUR CLOSET

· · · ·

THINK OF YOUR HOME AS A RETAIL STORE WITH UNSOLD INVEN-tory. Don't look any further than that. Your kid's toys. Clothes. Books. DVDs. Vinyl records. A car you don't use. Obsolete electronics that you can sell for the value of the parts. Americana (the prices here will surprise you). I want you to open up an eBay store, become a seller on Amazon, and sell your stuff. Be creative with descriptions; an old dress becomes "vintage fashion." Remember Tara Winter, the girl who started selling old Hollywood clothes on eBay when she was still a teenager? She is a genius marketer. Look up her online shop and learn from her.

Create a territory that's yours; once you're up and running, you can go to your neighbors and friends and family. Let them know you can sell their stuff online. Give them 60 percent of the proceeds; you keep 40 percent. You will be amazed at the steady flow of merchandise that comes your way once word gets out. You will also learn about pricing, marketing, and e-commerce in the process. It is good training for your next moneymaking enterprise. Work that entrepreneurial muscle.

You don't have time, you say? Do it for an hour or two a week, on the weekend. It does not have to take over your life. You can even set up your seller profile so that customers know you ship items only one day a week.

If you've never sold anything online, start with books on Amazon. No need to take photographs or write descriptive copy. Just set yourself up as a seller (find instructions at services.amazon.com) and type in the ISBNs of your books to list them. Set your selling price based on what other sellers are asking for the same title. And then set your price for one penny less. Do research on your competitors. How do they handle shipping? What would your shipping costs be? Would building them into your price and offering free shipping make your product more appealing?

Now put away every cent you make from your side business. Don't touch it; save it!

life-changing magic

Over the past year, I lost thirty pounds. It was the weight I put on when I went back to school. I worked hard to lose it, and it feels great to have that part of my life under control. Not long ago, I ventured into my closet to make sense of it. It was brimming with multiple sizes of clothes from the many phases of my life. It was time to clean it out.

It turned out to be a multiple-weekend endeavor and an emotional trip. I don't consider myself a super shopper, and yet I could not believe I'd collected so much stuff. It made me think about how much less we actually need or use than what we have, and how much buying clothes can be a quick fix that distracts you from big goals.

I'd read *The Life-Changing Magic of Tidying Up: The Japanese Art of Decluttering and Organizing*—a huge best seller—by Marie Kondo. Kondo describes the spiritual practice of clearing out all the useless stuff and clutter of your life in order to open yourself energetically to the new you, inside and out. I followed Kondo's instructions: I looked at every item in my closet, held it, tried it on, remembered every experience (good and bad), recalled every era—the 1980s, the 1990s, and beyond. I marveled when I found something old that looked chic and "vintage." I noted my "Jersey girl" phase, my "Texas cowgirl" phase, my "Boston grunge" phase, my "Hollywood glam" phase, my "female power suit" phase, my "TV anchorwoman" phase, and my back-to-school "all sweats/all the time" wardrobe.

I enjoyed and honored every phase, every version of me, and then I let them all go. Then I asked myself, "Who am I now? Who is the woman I have become?"

As women, we have to evolve and grow, honor our past, forgive our mistakes (and our wardrobe faux pas), and constantly search for who we are now. Today is all we have. Marie Kondo's book is such a phenomenon because it touches on an absolute truth: In order to keep growing, we have to clean out the past. The stuff we keep is a metaphor for something we hold on to that no longer serves us. Energetically, we must transform that past energy into generosity toward others by giving those things away to those who could use them or would enjoy them more, or we should turn them into money (remember, think of it as unsold inventory) and bring revenue to ourselves and our families.

I just started organizing my teenage son's room, and I have relived his entire childhood. I found some *Star Wars* toys that McDonald's gave out in its Happy Meals many years ago. They are now collector's items and are selling for upwards of five hundred dollars each. After I finish crying over my little baby being so grown up, my son and I are going to get down to business and make some money off Luke Skywalker and Darth Vader to put toward his college years.

there are many ways to become self-made.

WHILE YOU'RE MAKING SACRIFICES, LOWERING your overhead, funding your accounts, and learning to love saving money—all the things you need to do as you become self-made—you should be thinking about what kind of entrepreneur you want to be. What will your business be? What need will your business or your product meet in the marketplace? How will it catch on? And how do you come up with a business idea anyway? I have another three-step proposition to get you thinking:

> **Start.** We've got this covered—you've already
> started! You made a choice to be here with me,

right now. You're changing your mindset from instant gratification to goal orientation. You've
learned that what lies ahead will not be easy, but
you're making a commitment. You know that
tough things require stamina, but you're in, because the rewards are great.

Solve a problem. I tell the women I speak to, "Your
pain is the gateway to your most authentic
brand." Your pain identifies the problem you are
uniquely suited to solve. What is the problem?
What would solve the problem? How do you turn
that into a business?

Find an audience. Where are the people just like
you who share this problem? How can you find
them? Are they in your community? Online? Is it
a local or national need? What is the most effective way to reach out and let them know that you
have the solution?

THERE ARE MANY WAYS
TO GET YOUR OWN CHIPS!

· · · ·

WHAT KIND OF SELF-MADE WOMAN ARE YOU? AND WHAT KIND
of entrepreneurial business matches your skills? Here are
some pathways to consider.

SHARED-ECONOMY OPPORTUNITIES

THE DIGITAL ECONOMY PROVIDES ENORMOUS OPPORTUNITIES for entrepreneurs to sell their products, to market their businesses, to lower their overhead, and to work part-time or full-time from home. On-demand networking apps like Uber, Lyft, and TaskRabbit are part of a new wave of "shared economy" business platforms that use social media and mobile devices to enable ordinary people to leverage their skills, possessions, and talents into paying services. TaskRabbit, for example, works on a local level to connect those who are willing to do household chores and errands for cash with paying customers in their neighborhoods. TaskRabbit services range from handyman jobs and cleaning services to help with moving, shopping, and party planning. The virtual market for handcrafted goods is also growing. Sites like Etsy and Handmade at Amazon have tapped the appetite for everything from knitted socks and fancy doghouses to patchwork quilts, chili-pattern dishware, and antler coatracks. Want to market your flair for graphic design? You can do it with Folyo or Dribbble. Want to create and sell your own T-shirts? Check out Teespring. There's almost nothing you can do or make that doesn't have a monetary value to somebody somewhere, and the vast virtual marketplace at your fingertips makes connecting with your customers easier than it's ever been before.

Go to becomingSELFMADE.com to find a complete list of shared-economy opportunities.

I AM SELF-MADE: Melissa Paz

WHEN MELISSA PAZ WAS A RECENT COLLEGE grad, the job market in Puerto Rico was tight. Shortly after she got married, she and her husband emigrated to the United States in search of better opportunities. They settled in Florida and took entry-level jobs at Universal and Disney to pay the bills. Melissa moved on to positions at AT&T and Tupperware, but when the couple decided to start a family, Melissa wanted the freedom to be at home with her children. She started working in customer service for a bank—work that she could do from home—which was a great solution . . . until she was laid off. With two young children, she needed to find a way to bring in money right away.

Remembering how she'd made extra cash selling used textbooks on eBay during college, Melissa enlisted the help of her mother to find things around her home—used and new—that they might be able to sell on eBay. She set up an eBay shop, LazyBreeze Deals. The items sold surprisingly quickly, and the financial pressure on the family eased a bit, but Melissa realized that in order to grow and expand her business, she needed more stuff to sell. She started looking for liquidated clothing lots and began experimenting with different types of inventory.

She also realized that she needed to reach out to other sellers and learn from their experiences.

With this in mind, Melissa set up the eBay Sellers of Central Florida Meetup—a monthly meeting for eBay sellers in her area where seasoned experts could share tips and help newer sellers succeed. She learned how to choose and source inventory and how to market it. At one of her meetups, she met Danna Crawford, an eBay certified business consultant and power seller, who became her mentor and eventually connected her with a personal contact at eBay and helped her become a certified eBay influencer and ambassador.

Melissa used the advice of her online community to further refine her selling techniques and began working with companies that would take orders straight from her shop and ship directly to the buyers from their warehouses—a practice known as drop shipping. This meant that Melissa didn't have to bother with storing and shipping inventory. As she experimented with different products, she found that she had a knack for selling luggage, backpacks, and travel gear. She had always had a passion for travel, so she was able to choose her stock wisely and write selling descriptions of her inventory because she knew what features experienced travelers would be looking for. Being fluent in both Spanish and English, Melissa has also been able to tailor her shop to the Latino and bilingual market, specifically targeting an underserved community.

Melissa's success came quickly because she used the

wisdom of the eBay community. She works on her store anywhere between two and twelve hours a day. She is currently working with eBay to grow and expand eBay Latino.

TAKE ADVANTAGE OF
AN EMERGING OPPORTUNITY

EMERGING BUSINESSES OPERATE WITHIN THE PARTS OF THE ECON- omy that are growing the fastest. Emerging countries are countries whose economies are growing rapidly, which means they are buying more goods and products than other countries. The businesses they are buying from benefit greatly from that emerging market. The BRIC countries—Brazil, Russia, India, and China—are emerging economies, as are some economies in Africa and the Middle East. And, as noted earlier in the book, the Latina market is the largest emerging market in the United States.

Emerging markets and businesses are where statisticians and economists predict the highest growth over the next fifty years. The businesses in the United States that are seeing the most rapid growth are in the digital and energy sectors. The car industry is also seeing growth. Emerging sectors grow exponentially every year, and they are dynamic—they change all the time—which means there are always new opportunities.

In 2016, emerging businesses in the United States included

services for the baby boomer demographic (the biggest, wealthiest sector of the population), such as exercise training and instruction and physical therapy; technology and social media; services for the Latina, African American, and multicultural women's market; services that address women's health (which is becoming increasingly specialized); and boxed, curated subscription services for food and products.

INVENT A COMPANY, A PRODUCT, A TECHNOLOGY COMPANY

I GOTTA BE HONEST: THIS IS THE HIGHEST (MEANING HIGHEST-RISK and highest-reward) and most difficult way to become self-made. It's not for everybody. It requires a type A personality, with vision and drive to spare. It's hard to be the leader, but it might be just what you're looking for. The classic example in this category is the genius inventor Sara Blakely, who solved the age-old problem of panty lines, bulging tummies, and jiggly parts with modern fabric technology and turned Spanx into an empire (and a new word in our everyday vocabulary!). She also counts as a disrupter (see below), because she radically changed the underwear industry. Blakely's net worth is estimated at over one billion dollars.

DISRUPT AN EXISTING BUSINESS

A DISRUPTER COMES UP WITH A PRODUCT OR A WAY OF DELIV- ering a service that changes "business as usual." Uber changed the taxi industry and the way we get around in cities. Amazon changed the way we shop—by creating algorithms that factor in our purchases and interests and suggest other things we may like. The iPod disrupted the music industry and the way we buy and listen to music. Elon Musk and PayPal changed the way we pay for goods and services. Birchbox—a monthly subscription service that delivers curated beauty products to your door—disrupted the retail cosmetics industry. But women like you are disrupting things in smaller ways every day. Ivette Mayo, whom you'll meet below, is a great example of a disrupter. So you see, disruptive innovation doesn't have to be grand; it can be local and specific. It just has to work!

I AM SELF-MADE: Ivette Mayo

IVETTE MAYO WAS BORN IN PUERTO RICO. HER father was in the navy, and Ivette and her family were always moving as he changed posts. By the time she was eight, Ivette had attended thirteen different elementary schools all around the United States. At home, she always felt connected to her cultural heritage, but out in the world she felt as if she didn't belong to any community.

After spending twenty-five years in corporate America, working in banking and as a Latin American sales manager for Continental Airlines, Ivette decided to create a business that reflected who she was and where she was from. She found a problem that she and others experienced that she was uniquely qualified to solve.

Ivette was often disappointed when she went looking for greeting cards. "Every time I bought a card, I would always think, I could do this better," she says. So she created a bilingual card line, Yo Soy Expressions, that she sells online and in stores. Ivette disrupted the greeting card business by filling a hole in the market with something people wanted but couldn't find: culturally specific greeting cards.

Cards by Yo Soy Expressions have become my favorite, and when I give them, people always ask where they can get them. What I also love about Ivette is that although she left her corporate job, she still understood the difference between her mission and her money. Ivette runs an executive coaching business, which brings in the cash, while she is incubating her start-up card business, which I know will be very successful.

"Find your purpose and don't be deterred by a no," says Mayo. "Say 'thank you and get out of my way.'" Mayo advises her fellow entrepreneurs not to be afraid. If you don't have the money to fund your project, figure out a way to get it. "My grandmother would say, *'Si tu quieres, tu puedes'* ['If you want, you can'], and that mindset has given me the fuel for my courage."

BUY A FRANCHISE

YOU MAY BE THE KIND OF ENTREPRENEUR WHO IS NOT A CREATOR but a great executor. In this case, buying a franchise or an existing business could be right for you. A franchise is a great way to start a business with less investment, and with the know-how and the marketing support of other owners and the parent corporation behind you. Plus there are many companies, such as UPS, Subway, and 7-Eleven, that actively recruit women as franchise owners. Also, there are franchises in so many categories that might not be obvious to you—for example, yoga studios, tutoring for kids, healthy eating services. All these are growth areas.

I love franchises because they allow you to run your own business with some of the kinks already worked out, thanks to the experience of your predecessors. You may be able to buy an existing franchise from someone who is retiring or moving and who has already built a base for you to grow from instead of starting from scratch.

There's a range of fees to buy into a franchise—some are expensive; some are reasonable—but there are loans available from banks, the SBA, and even sometimes the parent company itself. But you will need to put some money down; the loan won't cover everything. It's like buying a house. Franchise deals are usually for ten or twenty years, so the way to think about it is to amortize that cost over the term of the franchise and it will seem less overwhelming. There are also operating costs and fees that go toward national marketing. The parent company will also expect you to run the franchise in keeping with its standards and values. The upside is, given all its data and analysts, the parent can pretty much predict how much money you're going to make.

The advantages of owning a franchise include the ability to buy at a bulk discount; you can share supplies with multiple stores that are buying the same products. In addition, you have the benefit of knowing what is selling and what isn't selling from other franchises. Plus, you benefit from national marketing—a charge to the business, as noted above, but it's marketing done by expensive, creative experts on an epic scale, not trial-and-error attempts at local marketing.

Franchises are a much easier way to start a business. Plus, you can get your whole family involved! Put your kids to work as your employees—you'll be sending them to business school at the same time! You can also form a partnership that buys the franchise together as a group, rather than as an individual. If I had to do my life over, I'd buy many franchises. I'd buy one, figure out how to run it, and then buy a lot of them.

I AM SELF-MADE: Maria Villar

MARIA VILLAR, A CUBAN IMMIGRANT, WAS WORK-
ing as a teacher in Denver when her mother-in-law became ill with both cancer and dementia. Maria and her
husband felt ill-equipped to handle her medical needs.
They began to look for an assisted-living facility that
could properly care for her but were dissatisfied with all
the options in their community. Instead, they started
looking for a caretaker or health aide who could look
after her mother-in-law in her own home, and in the
course of this search Maria came across a franchise
called Home Helpers.

Maria was impressed that the franchise had been
around for fifteen years and none of the franchises had
gone bankrupt. She used her knowledge as an economist
to evaluate the business and thought it would be a smart
venture. Plus, she liked the idea of being able to hire
competent staff and provide safety and security for people like her mother-in-law. The price of the franchise was
relatively reasonable, so she and her husband sold a few
stock options that they had to cover the initial fee. She
opened her Home Helpers franchise in July 2015. Today,
she has eighteen employees who care for senior citizens,
children with disabilities, and people in the early stages
of Alzheimer's and dementia.

Maria had never intended to be an entrepreneur, but her family's struggle led her straight to an emerging business. There will be a growing need for elder care as the baby boomer generation ages. In buying a franchise, Maria started with a tested business plan. Her family's experience as customers gave her the ability to put her own personal spin on the business. Maria loves what she does. She has great empathy for the families she's helping, having been there herself.

BUY AN EXISTING BUSINESS (AND ADOPT THE FORMER OWNER AS YOUR MENTOR)

LOOK AROUND YOU—LOOK AT ALL THOSE BUSINESSES IN YOUR community. All those businesses have owners, and at least some of those owners may one day be looking to sell. Like buying a franchise, this is a great way to avoid having to climb the mountain all by yourself. Buying an existing business means you start out with a customer base already in place—a huge advantage. You're saving yourself five to ten years of building a clientele.

Is there a business in your community or one owned by a friend or acquaintance whom you admire and that, in your wildest dreams, you wish were yours? Maybe it can be, one day. Many people build thriving businesses, but their kids are not interested in taking over, or there is not a natural person in line to cede the business to when they retire. All business owners want to feel as if they've built a legacy. Take an interest in the business. Take a job there, get experience, learn it from the inside, and let the owner know you are ready to be mentored. You may even be able to negotiate to have the former owner stay with you for a time, to mentor you and introduce you to his or her clients.

Pay attention to your circle of acquaintances; you will be alert to opportunities and hear about businesses that might be considering selling. Inquire with local businesses you'd love to own; you might be surprised to find who's ready to sell. Your local chamber of commerce would have an idea of who in the community will be selling the business. There are also small-business brokers—just like real estate brokers—who represent business owners looking to sell.

This also goes back to mapping your skill set, the puzzle of your life. What skills were standouts for you, and what business might they suggest you'd be successful at?

PARTNER WITH A FRIEND, A GROUP OF FRIENDS, OR YOUR FAMILY

YOU MAY WORK WELL IN A TEAM. CONSIDER FORMING A PARTnership that will start a business and become self-made together.

I just matched up two of my friends so they can do business together, and it was possibly the best blind date either of them ever had. I know they will also become dear friends.

They will be a blessing in each other's lives in so many ways, and they will also be able to make so much money together. They are better together than apart. Not everyone is meant to be an entrepreneur alone. Some people work better with others. Many of us are afraid to start a business alone, but if we just had a partner to be brave with us, we could reach the moon!

Sometimes becoming self-made does not have to be a lone journey. There are other women out there who can be the other half we are looking for, with complementary skill sets and contacts, who can make something happen. Sometimes that other person is right under your nose—a child, a sister, a cousin, a friend since grade school, or a new acquaintance. Sometimes you need to partner with another member of your community so you can better service that community; sometimes it's better to partner with someone outside your community who will help you service a bigger market. Open your mind to partnership. Buying in as a group, as noted above, is a great way to buy a franchise or an existing business.

One cautionary note: When you work with friends and family, I advise that you draw up an agreement before you begin that addresses what will happen if things go south and there's a falling-out. It's like a prenuptial agreement for business. That way you go in with eyes wide open. Business schools are now offering courses on how to run a family- or partnership-owned business while respecting boundaries. We now realize there is a science to this; it takes work, it doesn't just happen naturally, and it's better not to leave it to chance.

I AM SELF-MADE: Yahaira Núñez

Yahaira Núñez attended a New York Adelante event. She'd opened a women's clothing store called Lollipop, but she was struggling with a lot of overhead costs and was looking for guidance. The first steps she'd taken had been the right ones: She wanted to become an entrepreneur. She had saved up a good bit of money, quit her job, and started her own business. Yahaira would find exotic and unusual pieces for her customers and pair them with clothes the customer had in her closet, mixing old and new to create fresh and stylish looks. She was good at what she did, yet she was having trouble making the rent on her store.

My first question to her was, "What was your intention in starting the store?"

"I'm Dominican," she said by way of an answer. "I'm a really good stylist."

"Actually, it sounds to me like you're really more of a curator of fashion than a stylist. You're a great shopper too. You source these rare finds and take them directly to your customers. You know what's going to work because you know what's in their closets. So let me ask you, why do you need to work out of a store?"

Yahaira went too fast and she crashed. She needed

to go back and take baby steps in building her business. She had tried to make a generic, mainstream store—Lollipop? What was that?—that catered to everyone and in the process overlooked her particular expertise and her identity! Her strength was her ethnic, hippieish, hodgepodge look! I told her that her style sounded like a *sancocho*. A *sancocho* is a Dominican soup that is made from yesterday's leftovers; it becomes something spicy and delicious when new ingredients are added. "*Sancocho* style" was born! I advised her to close the retail store and start a website. She took my advice and launched a Sancocho Style YouTube channel and started making videos that showed her process, going through a woman's closet, telling her what works and what doesn't work, and then showing things this customer could buy that would really make an outfit come together like *wow*.

Today, in addition to the YouTube channel, she has a Facebook page for her business. She also has a business model that allows her to sell clothes and accessories and to charge for her services as a wardrobe consultant. She is now pursuing advertisers and sponsors on her YouTube channel and Facebook page, because she's getting significant traffic. She is running her business out of her house, and she is making a profit. She's a *sancocho* guru.

CREATING A BRAND ONLINE
AND MONETIZING IT

THIS IS THE SPACE WHERE THE TARAS, CRAFTY CHICAS, MIRACLE Wanzos, and *you* can graduate to in the digital economy. This is the domain of YouTube stars, Vine video creators— any social media platform that takes advertising. You create content online, you build a following, and that following allows advertisers and other brands to align with yours. Michelle Phan is the best example of this; she's made her YouTube makeup tutorials into an attractive destination for advertisers. The best starting point for this is blogging. You develop an area of expertise and build a following; then, once you have a sizable following, you seek sponsors.

I AM SELF-MADE: Candy Ramirez

CANDY RAMIREZ GOT HER LOVE OF BAKING FROM her grandmother. As a child in the small town of Douglas, Arizona, she was entranced watching her *abuelita* Nana Lupe create sweet treats in the kitchen. "Baking with my grandmother was a bonding thing," Candy recalls. "It was peaceful watching her. She was in her element."

At eighteen, Candy was an unemployed single mother. Without many options, she turned to what she knew best and started baking cakes to make ends meet. Her cakes were delicious and inventive, but she was embarrassed to ask for money, so she was giving them to family and close friends for free. She had taken the first step toward becoming an entrepreneur but lacked the confidence and direction she needed to become a full-fledged businesswoman. "I felt weak and undeserving," she admits. "I had to take care of my parents and my son. It was really hard to wake up every morning. I was very unhappy."

Candy realized that she had to find a way to make money off her talent. She had no real contacts in the business world, so she joined her local Hispanic Chamber of Commerce in 2014 and began attending networking mixers that introduced her to people. She attended lectures that taught her what it meant to choose yourself.

The chamber of commerce asked Candy to bake a cake for an Adelante event. Candy's expertise was in making cakes that looked like objects, and she made an Adelante-branded purse out of cake that looked so realistic I tried to pick it up by the handle when I saw it! People fell in love with her creation and immediately inquired about placing orders. Later that year, Candy's Cakes & More won the Small Business of the Year award from the chamber of commerce.

Candy took that momentum and ran with it. At many of the chamber of commerce lectures, the speakers insisted that social media was the most effective tool for growing small businesses. Candy had never thought of her social media skills as something that could help get her business attention and orders. For the first time, she saw baking as something that could take her beyond just making ends meet with skills that she already had. First, she declared herself a professional chef and a baker (instead of someone who "liked to bake"). Then she set up a website for Candy's Cakes & More. Once that was up and running, she turned all of her social media accounts—Instagram, Twitter, and Facebook—into business accounts and posted pictures of her creations online. She was proactive about connecting with the people she had met at the chamber of commerce on social media, and they were eager to support her. The orders started coming in.

Word spread and her business took off. Two years in, Candy's Cakes & More gained a loyal following that included local celebrities and athletes, which boosted her social media reach further. Candy has since expanded her offerings and conducts guest cake-baking classes as far away as New York City. "Now I get excited when I wake up," she says. "I see a shift in where I'm going, in a different direction of being able to do more of what I want and empowering others. I'm not in bed, angry and upset or depressed, because I love what I do. I'm dreaming even bigger now." She has a combined following of nearly thirty thousand social media fans. She has acquired sponsors that provide free baking supplies and support for her business, and her cakes have been featured in *Cake Masters Magazine*. She's increased the price of her cakes to better match the market rate, and her cakes are in high demand. She no longer needs to work extra jobs. Baking and running a business are all pieces of a fulfilling career she truly loves.

Candy's work does not stop with running her own business. She believes strongly in helping other bakers and provides support and free training through weekly YouTube and Instagram tutorials. After participating in Adelante, Candy even launched #QueenBeeBaker, a positive online mentoring movement to support and inspire other bakers.

WHO'S ON YOUR TEAM?

· · · ·

YOU'RE NOT GOING TO BE ABLE TO DO THIS ALONE. YOU NEED A team! Earlier in the book, we talked about the need to get support on your emotional journey to becoming self-made. I'm not sure you ever totally outgrow that need. Be it a life coach, a pastor, a shrink, a compassionate spouse or friend—or all of the above!—you need an emotional support system in place. You'll also come to rely on a group of experts who can provide you with expert guidance and information.

Who do you need on your team? I'd recommend a banker as soon as you get serious about saving money. It's important not to be afraid of your bank. Walk in and ask to speak to someone; start a relationship. Along the way, you'll also need an accountant, a realtor if you're investing in real estate, a mortgage broker, and an insurance broker, among others. How to find the right ones for you? There are professional agencies that certify many of these professionals; that's a good place to start. You don't want someone with dubious credentials. Ask friends for referrals. Ask a lot of questions; put the word out that you are seeking guidance. People, particularly older people, will usually be happy to share the knowledge they've gained from their own experience. The Self-Made website (becomingSELFMADE.com) has a resource section that will help you find the right members of your team.

go get the hidden money in america.

NEVER IN HISTORY HAS IT BEEN EASIER FOR WOMEN to live entrepreneurially. Never has there been such a good time to start a franchise or get tax breaks, subsidies, and rebates. We are ready to take our place in society as owners and leaders, not just as workers and followers. The best way to get out of survival mode and build wealth is through entrepreneurship. The rewards are immense. It is our moment.

But I gotta tell you: It pains me that one of the biggest things holding us back is a simple lack of information, what I call the knowledge gap. There are so many opportunities available to female entrepreneurs, but we don't know where to look for them. If we don't take advantage of these opportunities, in the form of grants, contracts, government programs, and private sector resources that specifically target women, we are leaving money on the table. Knowledge is a tool for making money and keeping money, and we need to educate ourselves. So let's go find the hidden money in America!

FIND MONEY IN YOUR HOME

• • • •

IN BUSINESS, RECEIVABLES ARE A COMPANY'S ASSETS OR SERVICES that have value, or simply money that is owed to you. In business, you don't want to be sitting on receivables. You want to collect those debts. Your home is full of receivables. There is money to be found in your home. Go on a treasure hunt. Do it with your kids. Make it fun. "Finders keepers!" Find all the gift cards you get for Christmas and birthdays. No matter what a clerk tells you, *gift cards never expire.* If someone tells you a gift card can't be honored, ask to speak to a manager and tell him or her what the store is doing is illegal. Because it is. You know why businesses love gift cards so much? Because 80 percent of gift cards never get redeemed! Spend these gift cards instead of cash, and you'll have that savings to put away.

More receivables: coupons, rewards programs, rebates to be cashed in. Frequent-flier points. Renegotiate your payment plans for your phone and cable bills and your car insurance.

Call in loans you made to friends and family. Review your credit card statements monthly, and make sure that returns are accounted for and there are no mistakes. File your medical insurance claims, and make sure you spend every cent in your medical savings account or flex spending account.

There's a fringe benefit to this exercise: It breeds an awareness about the money you spend at home and where there is waste. Plus, you make your life more orderly. This awareness and organization you'll need to run your business.

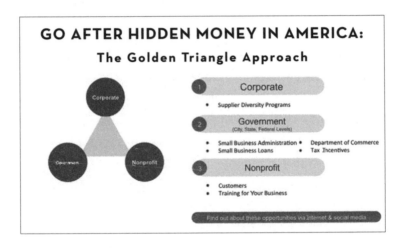

THE GOLDEN TRIANGLE

• • • •

THE "GOLDEN TRIANGLE" IS THE TERM THAT PEOPLE IN THE KNOW use to refer to the great, big secret hiding place for money in this country: corporations, the government, and nonprofits. Let's take a look at how to mine these pockets of opportunity.

CORPORATIONS

CORPORATIONS IN THE UNITED STATES OUTSOURCE A LOT OF their needs to outside suppliers. Everything from food—what the company cafeteria serves—to marketing and video production to supplying ingredients needed to create their product to printing, facility maintenance, and tech services comes from outside suppliers. Fortune 500 companies are encouraged by the federal government to give a percentage of their supplier contracts specifically to minority- and female-owned companies. These incentives also apply to products that companies sell to consumers. For example, Walmart is looking for women-owned businesses that can supply it with all kinds of products to sell in its stores. Top ranked among the companies with the biggest supplier diversity programs is the Coca-Cola Company. This is a point of pride for Coke, which takes it seriously and actively pursues minority- and female-owned companies.

How do you find out about these opportunities? Google "supplier diversity programs"!

You'll find a list of the kinds of products companies are looking for, and you'll find step-by-step guidance about how to be seen by buyers. These companies have local fairs across the country where you'll be invited to come in and pitch your product. If you are a woman, particularly a woman of color, they are looking to partner with you. If they are interested in your product but you're not able to meet the demands, they will try to pair you with a manufacturing partner. Walmart has one of the biggest supplier diversity programs around. If you get a Walmart contract to sell your products or your services, you have hit the jackpot because of the sheer volume.

For supplier diversity and government contracts (see below), you will be required to be certified: You have to prove that you are reliable and you are who you say you are. You have to be certified kosher! You'll find online a list of organizations in your state that offer certification. There is also a group called WIPP—Women Impacting Public Policy—that advises women on how to meet these standards and get certified. Getting in the door of these companies requires some work on your end—it's not a free ride by any means—but if you get it, boy, is it worth it.

THE GOVERNMENT

NEARLY EVERY DEPARTMENT OF THE FEDERAL GOVERNMENT OUT-sources work to third-party vendors in the form of government contracts. This means there's a lot of money for entrepreneurs in our government. For instance, a government office may have the need to produce training videos for its employees. If I'm a video producer, that's a contract I'd like to compete for. There are free classes all over the country that show us how to apply for government contracts. The problem built into these opportunities is that the government doesn't have the budget to market them, so the opportunity won't find you; you have to find it! Visit federal, state, and municipal websites and join their mailing lists.

As with supplier diversity programs, I'm not going to pretend it's easy to get through this door and become a gov-

GO GET THE HIDDEN MONEY IN AMERICA

ernment contractor. In some cases, it could take up to a year to pass the requirements and file all the paperwork, but if you are able to achieve this, it's a tremendous opportunity. On the Self-Made website, you will find stories of women who became government contractees. Trust me, it will inspire you!

Small Business Administration

THE SMALL BUSINESS ADMINISTRATION AND THE DEPARTMENT of Commerce have money for small-business owners. They have incredible loan programs for your business, they can help you to buy your company's office space, and they hold contests and forums for entrepreneurs all over the country.

The SBA has so many opportunities that are under the radar for most people. For example, if you buy a building for your company and you occupy at least 51 percent of it, you may be eligible for an SBA loan at a very low interest rate with very little money down. I wish I had known about this option when I started my first business. So many companies in America are worth less than the real estate they are sitting on! If you can, I encourage you to consider buying the building that houses your business. Go to sba.gov and learn about the many benefits the Small Business Administration offers, including training all across the country. You'll also find on the site the SBA offices near you where actual people can explain the ways you can take advantage of its offerings for your business. The SBA has an incredible website, full of resources. I encourage you to spend time exploring it.

Government Tax Incentives

THIS IS THE KIND OF NERDY SPENDER I AM: I PLAN MY YEAR AND
my big-ticket spending around the release of the federal government tax incentives in August. State tax incentives are announced throughout the year and often come in response to
a timely issue, such as environmental concerns or disasters.
Taking advantage of government tax incentives is like going
to the store with the biggest, richest stack of coupons you can
imagine.

The federal government stimulates emerging businesses by
creating tax incentives. Federal tax incentives are announced
in August on the IRS website. They are meant to stimulate
economic growth in industries that might be struggling. Plan
your big purchases accordingly. Here's an example from my
own life: Two years ago, I bought an SUV with a 75 percent
dollar-for-dollar tax incentive for buying cars of a certain
weight class. This means that on a fifty-thousand-dollar SUV,
I got 75 percent of the price of the car written off on my taxes.
The incentivized items change every year: One year, it's SUVs;
the next year, it might be solar panels or washers and dryers.
Don't make capital purchases for your family or business
without first checking for incentives. This is why financially
savvy people wait until the end of the year to make their big
purchases.

State tax incentives don't always match federal tax incentives. For example, because of drought conditions, California
offers people a tax incentive to replace their lawns with arti-

ficial turf. What does that tell you? Turf is an emerging business on the West Coast!

NONPROFITS

NONPROFITS ARE GREAT PARTNERS FOR ENTREPRENEURS. NON-profits will already have tapped into the audience you are looking for and can save you years of work by helping you target that audience. Let's say you are an accountant. If you advertise in the newsletter of a nonprofit that serves small businesses, it's targeted marketing. You can also donate to a nonprofit and take a tax write-off. Nonprofits are great sources of information and training that can help you close your own knowledge gap on a particular subject. Drill down into the wide variety of nonprofits that target women, African American women, Asian American women, or women with disabilities, for example. Find the affiliated group in your space or a related space and tap into its resources.

Nonprofits are also great landlords; renting space from a nonprofit is a great idea. They often rent office space that they got a deal on and look to supplement their organizational income by subletting unused office space at below-market rates. It's a win-win situation.

I AM SELF-MADE: # Monica Maldonado

MONICA MALDONADO'S FAMILY EMIGRATED FROM Colombia to Atlanta, Georgia, in 1982. Her family opened a small printing business. After graduating from college, Monica joined the family business as a sales representative. She and her father quickly became a dynamic sales duo—her father had the experience and knowledge, while Monica offered innovation and forward thinking—but about ten years in, their growth had stalled. They had been relying on small orders from retail and walk-in customers, inconsistent revenue sources that limited the shop's potential.

Monica assumed a larger role in the business and made some key decisions: She renamed the company Interprint Communications and decided to create a new business plan. She wanted to expand the business by targeting contracts from large commercial accounts and corporations. Looking for guidance, Monica joined the Georgia chapters of the National Minority Supplier Development Council (NMSDC) and the Women's Business Enterprise National Council (WBENC). There she learned about supplier diversity programs.

Since the business was based in Atlanta, Monica set her sights on the Coca-Cola Company—a company with enormous resources that was based in her city. In the hopes of becoming a printing supplier for Coke, she searched "supplier diversity, Coca-Cola" online and found a link where she could register.

Registering was easy, but actually becoming a supplier took time and determination. Monica had to fill out an intimidating amount of paperwork and become certified as a minority business owner. With the guidance of the WBENC, she was able to obtain minority certification.

Monica, who is now CEO and majority owner of Interprint Communcations, says, "The most important thing is to be persistent and not give up." Once she cracked the code of the supplier diversity applications, paperwork, and requirements, she was able to use her sales skills to pitch her services to Coca-Cola and successfully become a diversity supplier.

Landing a contract with Coca-Cola immediately took Monica's company to the next level. Coca-Cola began contracting with Interprint for a variety of smaller print projects and slowly moved the company to larger print and graphic design projects, allowing Monica time to grow and adapt her business to meet Coke's needs. Monica believes that it's just as important to set your business up to exceed customers' expectations as it is to be honest and forthright about your limitations, especially when taking big contracts. As Coke came to her with more demanding jobs, she recognized that to manage those orders she needed to be flexible and open to partnering with corporations that had the infrastructure she lacked. Her willingness to change and grow has kept her at the top of Coke's supplier list.

Interprint's revenue has grown by more than 30 percent every year since she became certified and landed her first contract with the Coca-Cola Company, but Monica's focus always remains on consistency and customer satisfaction. Interprint was able to invest more than $2 million in new facilities, a six-color press, and several other upgrades, all of which allow it to provide a superior product and faster printing times. Providing Coke with reliable service has led other companies to her door; Interprint now has supplier contracts with national companies such as AT&T, BMW, CNN, and Home Depot. Monica's vision, persistence, and hard work have grown the print shop from a small, family-run business to a company that has an annual revenue in the millions.

WINNING THROUGH CONTESTS

• • • •

CORPORATIONS, THE GOVERNMENT, AND NONPROFITS SPONSOR contests for women entrepreneurs throughout the year. An example of this is the Make Mine a Million $ Business contest sponsored by Count Me In that made a big difference in Rupila Sethi's life. Contests are a way to earn start-up money that you don't have to pay back. The winnings are a prize, not a loan. It's free money! Plus they afford you increased visibility for your product or business and publicity. And winning that prize is a certification that you can market with. You are a winner! Or a finalist! You have a ribbon or a seal! That's an awesome statement that you can take to market.

I AM SELF-MADE: Tatiana Birgisson

A S THE CHILD OF IMMIGRANTS, TATIANA BIRGIS-
son knew the value of an education. She worked hard
and got into a good school—Duke—and studied chemical
engineering in order to find a well-paying job after graduation.

While at Duke, Tatiana stayed up late and pulled all-
nighters to get her work done. She was living in a
university-funded residential apartment for undergradu-
ates interested in entrepreneurship, InCube, on Duke's
campus. Living and socializing with other people interested in becoming self-made planted a seed in her mind.
She was a big tea drinker, and she found that she was
brewing tea two or three times a day to keep her energy
up and get through her work. "Eventually, I got tired of
brewing tea multiple times a day, so I just started making
it all at once in a big pot in my dorm kitchen," she said.

Her tea became very popular with her fellow students. It was made of maté, an herb from South America.
(Tatiana's mother was Venezuelan, which is how Tatiana
knew about it.) The tea not only kept her alert without
getting jumpy; it also helped with bouts of depression
and homesickness. She thought she could market her
tea if she were able to turn it into an energy drink.

Birgisson spent a summer perfecting her recipe,

eventually deciding to use *guayusa* leaves, a close cousin to maté with nearly as much caffeine as coffee. After she figured out the best brewing method, Birgisson held tastings with her friends to nail down the best ratio of tea to fruit juice. She purchased a larger pot and moved the brewing operation to a communal kitchen.

"At first, I just sold it in kegs to offices," she said. "But then everyone began requesting it in cans so they could take some home and share it with their family." So Tatiana entered the Duke Start-up Challenge and won $11,500. She used that money to produce the drink in cans.

In 2015, twenty-five-year-old Tatiana Birgisson, founder of a new beverage company called MATI Energy, was one of four women to present at Google Demo Day, the annual event where Google invites entrepreneurs to pitch their start-ups to local investors and industry watchers. MATI Energy took the top prize and got lots of press coverage, including a story in *Forbes*. The *Forbes* story attracted investors, and MATI is now carried in six Whole Foods stores in the South, where it became a best seller in the category, and there are plans to roll it out to stores nationwide.

There are contests that can help get your business started all around the country. Tatiana learned about the Google contest through Duke, but you can find a complete listing of contests on the Self-Made app. Contests are like the *American Idol* of entrepreneurship, and they can help you home in on what your business is and help you present your concept in front of others. Plus, the winnings come with no strings attached; you don't have to pay anyone back, and you aren't selling off shares of your company. It's a great jump start.

Tatiana still does all the grunt work, from labeling cans, to taking orders, to delivering boxes. She says, "MATI will be carried in at least a hundred Whole Foods stores by the end of the year. I can see us going national in five years, maybe international. But I have to hire some more people first."

RAISING CAPITAL

· · · ·

AFTER TATIANA WON THE GOOGLE CONTEST, SHE TOOK ADVAN-tage of the publicity and buzz to solicit first-round investors in her company. Raising capital is the next stage of scaling a business. When you're ready to raise funds, go to the Self-Made website, where you'll find all kinds of guidance and resources about the best ways to take this on.

live a rich life in every way.

I HAVE BEEN ON THE ROAD FOR THE PAST FOUR YEARS meeting, speaking to, and training women in entrepreneurship, and I have had the privilege of taking many inspirational women on the road with me. One of those women is Rigoberta Menchú, the Nobel Peace Prize laureate, who has helped me understand and visualize what it means to be self-made every day. Rigoberta is an indigenous woman from Guatemala. When she was young, she lived in the mountains at a time when guerrilla warfare raged throughout the country and the indigenous people were being wiped out. Every Sunday, her father would walk her to a convent six hours away where she would work as a maid all week, and then at the end of the week her father would come and pick her up. Eventually, she learned to walk back and forth by herself.

Rigoberta did such good work that the nuns in the convent took a liking to her. At first, she spoke only an indigenous dialect, but the nuns taught her Spanish, as well as how to read and write. Once they could communicate, she was able to tell them the horrible things that were happening to her tribe. When she was a teenager, most of Rigoberta's family was massacred by guerrilla terrorists while she was at the convent. Fearing for her safety, the nuns smuggled her out of the country to a convent in Mexico.

When she got to the Mexican convent, Rigoberta told her story to one of the priests, who brought a team of journalists from France to interview her for two months straight. Those recordings turned into *I, Rigoberta Menchú,* a book that described in detail what was happening to the indigenous people of Guatemala and throughout Latin America. Her book was published in sixty languages around the world. She was awarded the Nobel Peace Prize in 1992 at the age of thirty-three.

I was blessed to be able to take Rigoberta on the road with me to talk to women in America. I wanted them to hear her moving, dramatic, incredible story and to be inspired by how much she was able to accomplish despite the obstacles she'd faced. She told the women, "If I could win the Nobel Peace Prize after starting out as a maid who couldn't even read, then you too can accomplish great things. What is your excuse, living in the United States with all these gifts and advantages you have?"

She also told me something that struck a deep chord within me and that has grounded me in this work. I try to echo it when I speak to women myself. She said, "The indigenous Guatemalan people believe that we must all wear a belt to remind us that half of us is of the sky and the other half of us is of the earth. Every day when we wake up, we need to remind ourselves of the highest dream we have, because without our dreams we are nothing. We have to think so big and so expansively and imagine things that we think are not possible. Then we have to remind ourselves that those dreams must be brought down into the earth, because we are also of the earth. Dreams without actions are nothing; they evaporate."

What is it that we need to do every day? We need to take our dreams, and we need to ground them in reality. We need to take concrete steps. As Rigoberta says, "Take the first step and plant the seeds. Do it every day."

I live by Rigoberta's words, and I put my own spin on them to describe what I do: I am a farmer. I love rolling up my sleeves and getting my hands dirty. I don't just plant the seed. I plow the fields. I water the sprouts. I am in the fields every day doing the work, and then in time my crop grows.

In the end, the money you earn is great, but it's not the big payoff. The payoff is that you know you can do this; you are strong inside, and you have real self-esteem built from the inside out, brick by brick, step by step. You've done every job along the way, and you've owned it at every stage. You could do it all over again if you had to. You can replicate your success because it comes from within you. Plus, you'll do it faster and better next time because you have all that experience under your belt. And you are ready to share what you've learned with others. It doesn't get any bigger than that. You are now empowered, self-reliant, and rich in every way. Congratulations!

PASSING THE TORCH

• • • •

WHAT IS OUR GREATEST INTENTION AS WOMEN? WE CARRY THE seed of future generations—both literally and figuratively. One of our deepest urges we have as women is to bring new life into the world. Even those of us who choose not to have children, or who can't have them, are born with a maternal instinct. It is our nature to nurture, to take care of the ones we love. For a very long time, that was all we needed to give our lives direction and deeper meaning. But it is no longer enough. We are ready and able to do more.

It's not that loving our spouses and children and raising a family have lost their meaning. It's actually just the opposite. It's because we want to create better lives for our families, our communities, and ourselves. We are able to create new pathways, to right the wrongs of past generations, to blaze new and better trails for future generations. It's the prize of the heroine's journey.

Should you ever think that what you're doing on your self-made journey is selfish—and you may well hear that—here is what I want you to hold tight and be very clear about within yourself: This journey is not just about you. You are leading by example. You are creating a new model for your daughters and their daughters. You are modeling behavior for your sons when they choose wives. Your grandchildren will say, "My grandmother was an entrepreneur, and she kicked ass." You are raising a generation to be self-made, not entitled. You are changing the world around you.

As Rigoberta Menchú says, we farm and we plant little seeds every day that will blossom and grow. Becoming self-made is the legacy that you leave for your children, your family, your community. Self-made can become something bigger than we are. We are planting seeds that are grounded in the earth and that blossom into dreams that reach for the sky.

CLIMBING THE PYRAMID

• • • •

SEVERAL YEARS AGO, I TOOK A TRIP TO MEXICO WITH A GROUP of friends, and we went to visit the important ancient archaeological site Teotihuacán, a pre-Columbian city located outside Mexico City that dates back to the first half of the first millennium. Teotihuacán, known as "the birthplace of the gods," was built by the members of a mysterious civilization, older than the Mayas and the Aztecs, who came to worship their ancestors at temples decorated with carvings dedicated to the god Quetzalcoatl, the Plumed Serpent, who symbolizes the link between the earthbound world of men and the realm of divine deities that live in the sky above. It's a very sacred place.

The tallest structure in Teotihuacán is the Pyramid of the Sun, the third-largest pyramid in the world, built around A.D. 200. The stone stairs of the pyramid rise 233 feet almost straight up. Climbing it is a killer; it's hot under the baking sun, the stone steps are rough, and the ascent is steep and vertical. But climbing the pyramid is one of the great things to do in Mexico, so up we go.

There's a way station just before you reach the top, where we stop to take a drink and catch our breath for the final ascent. It's very windy—apparently, it's always windy up there—and you feel as if you were going to fall off the pyramid. We drink our water, trying not to look down.

Our guide says, "Most people never reach the top because the wind scares them. They either give up and go back down or they fall over the edge." He laughs—maybe not the best joke because some tourists have, in fact, died from falling down the steps. He continues, "The secret to reaching the top is not being afraid of the wind and not being afraid that you will fall. You are the one who stops you from going higher. The wind is not going to topple you. *You* will topple you over."

And with those words, I take his challenge and join the group that will keep climbing, step by step, in the wind and the heat. And that way, I reach the top. I take in the panoramic, breathtaking view and wonder why I ever thought I couldn't make it. *Wow—I get it!* The metaphor gets at a profound truth: You are the real obstacle.

Achieving the self-made dream happens step-by-step, every minute of every day of your life. And even when you are within reach of your goal, there's the wind; the wind is always blowing. But you have what it takes to make it. And when you do, you'll wonder what made you think you couldn't. Take it all in, enjoy every minute of your achievement, and then, trust me, you'll start looking around for the next peak. Because you're hooked. You're ready for the next challenge. Just ask me. I'm still climbing.

**SELF
MADE**

Tell us your self-made story and find
the stories of other self-made women at

becomingSELFMADE.com

Download the free SELF MADE companion
mobile app for iOS and Android.

www.becomingSELFMADE.com/app

acknowledgments

I WANT TO THANK GUY GARCIA, WHO BECAME MY FRIEND after trailing me for an article he wrote for *The New York Times Magazine*. That article was a major moment in my life. I followed his career as a journalist at *Time, The New York Times,* and AOL and admired his books *The New Mainstream* and *The Decline of Men,* amazed at his accuracy in predicting trends. His research led him to join EthniFacts, a research and statistics firm that predicts cultural and societal waves for Fortune 500 companies. I enlisted his help with this book because I knew that Self-Made was a cultural and economic shift and I wanted to ground it in the data. I am excited that a groundbreaking research report has been created, based on the work he did for this book, called "The Self-Made Economy." This report explains the surge in female entrepreneurship, particularly among multicultural women, and its impact on the national and global economies.

Thank you, Guy, for an incredible experience working in a stunning Catskills setting, talking and capturing stories. I am so grateful that you got me started on my maiden voyage. You made the very emotional experience of writing a book beautiful. I also would like to thank Lisa Quiroz, Guy's wife and my dear friend, for so generously opening your home to me.

Thank you to Julie Grau, my editor and publisher, whom I met way back when *Entertainment Weekly* included us on a list of "people to watch," about up-and-coming execs in the entertainment industry. I boldly wrote her a letter telling her I thought her job was cool and that we should meet. We became friends, marking each other's important life events over the years. It was a full-circle moment to work together and be able to share so much of our journeys. Julie, thank you so much for your hard work, for sprinkling magical fairy dust on my words, and for helping me find my voice as a writer. I know this has been an experience neither of us will ever forget.

Thank you to the Random House team: Tom Perry, Cynthia Lasky, Sally Marvin, Melanie DeNardo, Leigh Marchant, Andrea DeWerd, Jessica Sindler, Steve Messina, and Barbara Bachman. Thanks to Greg Mollica for my beautiful jacket. Special thanks to Laura Van der Veer for working nights and weekends. I so appreciate your commitment.

I want to thank Mim E. Rivas and Todd Nordstrom for getting me started with their loving support, and Joanne Gordon for helping me find the *why*.

Thank you to my literary agents, Jan Miller and Lacy Lynch. Jan, from the minute I knew I wanted to do this book, I wanted to work with you. I admire your self-made story so much. You are an exceptional person and an extraordinary businesswoman. I will definitely be channeling you in one of my "act as if" moments. Lacy, you are a fierce warrior and an uber-intelligent young woman. I have loved every minute of working with you. You are committed and powerful and I am so happy to have you on my team. I look forward to watching you become. . . .

Heidi Krupp, thank you for your help with the publicity for the *Self Made* book and brand. I love your positive energy. You are a rock star. Your incredible team—Gabrielle Aboodi, Caity Cudworth, and Darren Lisiten among them—have my deepest appreciation.

Gabriel Reyes was the assistant I told to become a publicist, so I fired him as my assistant and hired him as the Galán Entertainment publicist. Thank you for helping me so much over the years. I love you dearly.

Natalie Molina Niño is a tech start-up maven and a great friend. Thank you for bringing your talents and your amazing team to the Self-Made brand strategy. Special thanks to Rakia Reynolds, Citi Medina, Joya Dass, Almaz Crowe, and Sheena Allen. And a big thank you to Bonny Taylor.

Monica Haim, thanks for helping once again, this time overseeing all the content for the Self-Made website. I thank you and wonderful Aaron for your love and support.

To Ingrid Duran and Catherine Pino, Roberto Fierro, Anais Carmona, and the rest of the D.C. team, you have all my appreciation.

Steven Wolfe Pereira—a special thank you to my twin. We have been dear friends ever since we met. Your love, support, and brainpower have been invaluable to me. Thank you for the many hours we've spent creating. . . . A special shout-out to Nuria and Sebastian. So happy you landed the plane.

Suze Orman, you are a committed supporter of women. Thank you for your generosity. You are truly authentic and congruent and that is why I follow your lead.

Sandra Cisneros, you are a true friend and an inspiration. I treasure the time we've spent together and I thank you for teaching me to find my authentic voice and to become a *chingona*.

Nell Merlino, you are a generous soul who has given so much to women. You inspire me every day to be a better person. Without your leadership there would be no Adelante Movement and no Self-Made.

Jay Itzkowitz, thank you for being my trusted advisor and friend. I love our breakfast-napkin business plans. Thank you, Pria, for your love and support as well.

To my team at Galán Entertainment: Rob Smith, thank you for having my back at all times, for your loyalty and your calm. Danila Koverman, whom I have known since she hired me at E!, thank you for organizing and executing our entire digital life. Luisa, I am happy to have you on board. Michael Gloistein, thank you for keeping our books together. Roberta and Ted Turner, my accountants for years, thank you for being my solid backbone.

To Sheila Conlin, Tim Ferretti, and Dave Downey: thank you for making the Self-Made stories come to life.

Special thanks to Concepción Lara, who believed in me, even in my darkest moments, and to Diana Mogollon, Kathleen Bedoya, Barbara Farmer, Carlos Portugal, and Norma Carballo, the original Galán team. You are my family.

To my agents and friends at WME—Mark Itkin, who believed in me and supported me for more than twenty-five years (you will be missed), Jad Dayeh, and Angela Petillo, with whom I love doing deals—I thank you all.

Thank you to the women who inspire me, my mentors, and my friends: Supreme Court justice Sonia Sotomayor, U.S. Treasurer Rosie Rios, Maria Contreras-Sweet, Janet Murguía, Nina Vaca, Linda Dunn, Sheryl Sandberg, Arianna Huffington, Gayle Berman, Sherry Lansing, Patti Rockenwagner, Dawn Ostroff, Maria Elena Lagomasino, Rigoberta Menchú, Andrea Robinson, Diane Forden, Monique Pillard, Dottie Franco, Diana Alverio, Aida Barrera, Raysa Bonow, Bea Stotzer, Minerva Madrid, Anne Thomopoulos, Patssi Valdez, Pam Colburn, Deborah Groening, Elaine Spierer, Luisa Liriano, Kelly Goode, Janet Yang, Debra Martin Chase, Sheila Conlin, Karen Koch, Donna Groves, Maggie Langley, and Susan Habif.

Thank you to the men who have mentored me, inspired me, and helped me out over the years: Bob Regan, Henry Cisneros, Raul Yzaguirre, John Oxendine, Bernard Stewart, Michael Solomon, David Salzman, Emilio Azcárraga, Michael Fuchs, Chris Albrecht, Lowell Mate, David Evans, Rich Battista, Haim Saban, Rupert Murdoch, Jon Feltheimer, Andy Kaplan, Alan Sokol, Don Browne, Jim McNamara, Mike Darnell, Ben Silverman, Chuck LaBella, Cris Abrego, Jeff Zucker, Gary Acosta, Armando Tam, Mel Cooper, Rene Alegria, Jerry Perenchio, Al Erdynast, John Langley, and Frank Ros.

I want to thank my friends at the Coca-Cola Company and the Coca-Cola Foundation who have supported my work with the Adelante Movement: Sandy Douglas, Lauventria Robinson, Bea Perez, Kathleen Ciaramello, Monica McGurk, Lori Billingsley, Linda Brigham, Alba Adamo, Sarah Marske, Angie Rozas, April Jordan, Lillian Rodríguez López, Rudy Beserra, Humberto García-Sjögrim, Peter Villegas, Reinaldo Padua, Melissa Palacios, and Alejandro Gomez.

To my family—my loving parents and my brother, Arsenio; my aunts, Dulce, Rosa, and Adelita; and the family in Cuba, Nina, Georgina, my uncle, José Manuel, and my cousins, Maritza, Elena, Emily, Yvette, and Chevy—thank you for loving me unconditionally. To my stepson Paul (P-Rod), I have known you since you were eight years old and I am so proud of the self-made man you have become. To Paul, thank you for giving me the greatest gift in my life, Lukas. To Teresa, whom I loved so much and miss so much. My love to the entire Rodriguez family for their love and support. To my "modern family": Thanks to the Ulfs for welcoming Lukas and me into the family fold in such a loving way. Thank you to Betsy and Frank Ulf for the many beautiful times we have shared, and to my stepkids Amanda, Abby, and Connor for your openheartedness, love, and laughs.

To my little nuclear family: Brian, Lukas, and Desi the Yorkie. Thank you for all the love.

Finally, to all my Adelante women, who have inspired this book, and to all my Latina, African American, Asian American, Native American, Middle Eastern American, and White sisters: I have quantum compassion for all of us. Our journeys are never easy, but this is the moment for us to reach and to grow. We are all in this together.

ABOUT THE AUTHOR

Dubbed the "Tropical Tycoon" by *The New York Times Magazine*, NELY GALÁN is a women's empowerment advocate, an Emmy Award–winning television producer, and the owner of Galán Entertainment, a dynamic, multicultural media company that has created more than seven hundred television shows in English and Spanish and helped launch ten channels around the world. The first Latina president of a U.S. television network, Telemundo, Galán is also the founder of the Adelante Movement, a national motivational tour and digital platform that unites and empowers Latinas socially, economically, and politically. She is a sought-after speaker who has spoken at the Coca-Cola Company, American Express, JPMorgan Chase, General Electric, the Clinton Foundation, and the United Nations, among other companies and organizations.

nelygalan.com

becomingSELFMADE.com

Facebook.com/Becomingselfmade

@beSelfMadenow

ABOUT THE TYPE

This book was set in Sabon, a typeface designed by the well-known German typographer Jan Tschichold (1902–74). Sabon's design is based upon the original letter forms of sixteenth-century French type designer Claude Garamond and was created specifically to be used for three sources: foundry type for hand composition, Linotype, and Monotype. Tschichold named his typeface for the famous Frankfurt typefounder Jacques Sabon (c. 1520–80).